From Scarcity to Abundance: Mastering the Art of Instantaneous Gratitude for a Wealthy Mindset.

FROM SCARCITY TO ABUNDANCE

First edition. March 13, 2024.

Copyright © 2024 Gonzalo Estrada.

ISBN: 979-8224337576

Written by Gonzalo Estrada.

Table of Contents

Contents

Chapter 1: The Power of Gratitude

In our fast-paced world where we often find ourselves chasing after more, it's easy to overlook the importance of gratitude. But what if we told you that cultivating a mindset of gratitude could unlock a wealth of abundance in your life? The power of gratitude is truly transformative, and in this chapter, we will explore its incredible effects and guide you on a journey toward mastering the art of instantaneous gratitude for a wealthy mindset.

Gratitude is more than just a polite gesture or a way to express appreciation. It is a fundamental shift in our perspective, allowing us to recognize and embrace the abundance that already exists in our lives. When we shift our focus from scarcity to abundance, we open ourselves up to a world of possibilities and attract more positive experiences.

Practicing gratitude begins with a simple mindset shift. It's about consciously choosing to see the blessings that surround us, even in the smallest of moments. Take a moment right now to reflect on something you are grateful for. It could be as simple as a warm cup of coffee in the morning or a heartfelt conversation with a loved one. By acknowledging these moments of gratitude, we plant the seeds for a mindset of abundance to flourish.

One of the transformative effects of gratitude is its ability to shift our perspective from lack to sufficiency. When we constantly focus on what we don't have, we create a sense of scarcity in our lives. This scarcity mindset keeps us trapped in a constant state of wanting more, believing that happiness lies in the next achievement or possession. However, by cultivating gratitude, we begin to see the abundance that already exists. We realize that we are enough and that our lives are filled with countless blessings.

Practicing gratitude also has a profound impact on our overall well-being. Research has shown that individuals who regularly practice gratitude experience increased levels of happiness, lower levels of stress, and improved mental health. When we focus on what we are grateful for, our brains release dopamine and serotonin, also known as the "feel-good" chemicals, which uplift our mood and promote a sense of well-being. By shifting our attention to the positive aspects of our lives, we create a ripple effect of positivity and joy.

Furthermore, gratitude fosters deeper connections with others. When we express gratitude, whether through a simple thank you or a heartfelt note, we not only acknowledge someone's kindness but also strengthen our relationships. Gratitude cultivates a sense of appreciation and reciprocity, opening doors for more meaningful connections and fostering a supportive environment.

But how do we cultivate a mindset of gratitude in a world that often encourages us to focus on what we lack? The key lies in daily gratitude practices. These practices act as reminders for us to shift our focus and embrace the abundance that surrounds us. Whether it's keeping a gratitude journal, practicing meditation, or expressing gratitude to others, these small acts create a ripple effect in our lives and transform our mindset.

As you embark on this journey toward mastering the art of instantaneous gratitude, we invite you to reflect on the transformative power of gratitude in your own life. Take a step back and appreciate the blessings that already exist. Embrace the abundance that surrounds you. Throughout this book, we will delve deeper into the practices and techniques that will enable you to cultivate a wealth mindset through the power of gratitude.

Remember, gratitude is not just an occasional act but a way of life. In the second part of this chapter, we will explore practical strategies to incorporate gratitude into your daily routines and uncover the true potential it holds. So, keep reading and get ready to unleash the power of gratitude in your life.

This is not the conclusion of the chapter. The second part will be continued in the next section.) In the second part of this chapter, we will delve deeper into the practical strategies and techniques that will enable you to cultivate a wealth mindset through the power of gratitude. So, let's continue our journey of discovering the transformative effects of gratitude and learn how to incorporate it into our daily routines.

One powerful way to embrace gratitude is through the practice of keeping a gratitude journal. This simple yet effective technique involves writing down three things you are grateful for every day. It could be anything, from the warmth of the sun on your skin to the kind words of a friend. By consciously acknowledging and appreciating these moments of gratitude, we begin to shift our focus from what's lacking to the abundance that already exists in our lives.

Another practical strategy to cultivate gratitude is to engage in meditation. Taking a few moments each day to cultivate a state of mindfulness allows us to become fully present and aware of the blessings surrounding us. During your meditation practice, focus on your breath and silently repeat affirmations of gratitude. For example, you can say, "I am grateful for the love and support in my life" or "I am grateful for the opportunities that come my way." By incorporating gratitude into your meditation practice, you create space for a wealth mindset to flourish.

Expressing gratitude to others also plays a crucial role in cultivating a mindset of abundance. Take a moment each day to express appreciation to someone in your life. It could be a simple thank you note, a heartfelt text message, or even a verbal expression of gratitude. Not only does this practice strengthen your relationships, but it also fosters a sense of appreciation and reciprocity. By spreading gratitude, you contribute to a supportive and uplifting environment.

In addition to these daily practices, it is essential to cultivate an attitude of gratitude throughout the day. This means being mindful of even the smallest moments and finding something to be grateful for in each of them. Whether it's savoring a delicious meal, appreciating a beautiful sunset, or finding joy in the laughter of a child, there are countless opportunities to practice gratitude every day. By training ourselves to look for these moments, we develop a habit of seeing the abundance that surrounds us.

As you continue on your journey toward mastering the art of instantaneous gratitude, it's important to be patient and gentle with yourself. Cultivating a mindset shift takes time and practice, but the rewards are immeasurable. Remember that every step you take in the direction of gratitude brings you closer to a wealth mindset and a life filled with abundance.

In the fast-paced world we live in, it's easy to get caught up in the pursuit of more. However, by embracing gratitude, we unlock the power to transform our lives and shift our focus from scarcity to abundance. The practice of gratitude not only enhances our overall well-being but also fosters deeper connections with others and creates a ripple effect of positivity and joy.

So, as you conclude this chapter, take a moment to appreciate the progress you've made so far. Reflect on the transformative power of gratitude in your own life and the positive changes you've experienced. Embrace the abundance that surrounds you, and keep practicing the techniques and strategies we've explored.

Remember, gratitude is not just an occasional act but a way of life. It is through daily practices and a conscious shift in mindset that we truly cultivate a wealth mindset. So, continue reading, keep learning, and unleash the power of gratitude in your life. The journey toward abundance starts with gratitude, and you have taken the first step.

Chapter 2: The Scarcity Mindset: Recognizing the Block

In our quest for abundance and a wealthy mindset, it is essential to first recognize the obstacles that may be holding us back. One of the biggest hurdles that prevent us from achieving true abundance is the scarcity mindset. Without even realizing it, many of us fall victim to this detrimental mindset, which can hinder our growth and limit our potential.

The scarcity mindset is deeply rooted in fear and a sense of lack. It is characterized by a belief that resources are limited, opportunities are scarce, and there is never enough to go around. Individuals trapped in this mindset operate from a place of constant worry, always afraid of not having enough, whether it be money, time, or success.

This scarcity mindset manifests itself in various ways in our lives. It can be seen in the belief that there is only one path to success or that others' accomplishments diminish our own chances. It fills our minds with thoughts of competition, comparison, and envy, creating a toxic cycle that keeps us stuck in a mentality of scarcity.

At its core, the scarcity mindset thrives on the idea that there is not enough for everyone. It blinds us to the abundance that surrounds us and prevents us from appreciating the blessings already present in our lives. This distorted perception not only limits our ability to attract more abundance but also robs us of the joy and fulfillment that come with practicing gratitude.

To break free from the scarcity mindset, we must first become aware of its presence in our lives. Pay attention to your thoughts and emotions when it comes to money, success, and opportunities. Do you find yourself constantly worrying about not having enough? Are you frequently comparing yourself to others and feeling inadequate? These are telltale signs of a scarcity mindset.

Next, it is essential to challenge the scarcity mindset's underlying beliefs. Recognize that abundance is not a finite resource, but rather a state of mind. Embracing this belief opens up a world of possibilities and allows us to tap into the infinite potential within us. Cultivating an abundance mindset means understanding that opportunities are abundant, success is not limited, and there is enough for everyone to thrive.

Practicing gratitude is a powerful tool in shifting from scarcity to abundance. When we consciously focus on the blessings in our lives, we invite more of them to flow into our experience. By appreciating what we have instead of constantly striving for what we lack, we change our perspective and attract more abundance into our lives.

It is also important to surround ourselves with like-minded individuals who embody an abundance mindset. Seek out those who uplift and inspire you, who believe in limitless possibilities and encourage you to step outside of your comfort zone. By surrounding ourselves with positive influences, we create an environment conducive to growth and abundance.

Recognizing and overcoming the scarcity mindset is a transformative journey that requires consistent effort and self-reflection. It is not an overnight process, but with persistence and dedication, we can break free from its grip and embrace a mindset of abundance. In doing so, we open ourselves up to a world of infinite possibilities, where success, joy, and fulfillment flow effortlessly into our lives.

...In our journey toward transforming our mindset from scarcity to abundance, it is crucial to recognize the impact that a scarcity mindset can have on our daily lives. The first half of this chapter explored the various ways in which this detrimental mindset manifests itself in our thoughts and actions. Now, let's delve deeper into how we can break free from its grip and cultivate a mindset of abundance.

One powerful practice that can help us shift from scarcity to abundance is the art of reframing our thoughts. When we catch ourselves slipping into negative thought patterns rooted in lack and limitation, we have the opportunity to reframe those thoughts into ones of gratitude and abundance. For example, instead of dwelling on lack and worrying about not having enough, we can choose to focus on what we do have and express gratitude for it. By actively choosing to see the abundance in our lives, we begin to attract more of it.

Another way to cultivate an abundance mindset is through visualization. Take a moment to close your eyes and imagine yourself living a life of abundance. See yourself surrounded by all the blessings you desire, whether it be financial wealth, fulfilling relationships, or personal success. Visualize yourself already experiencing these blessings, and feel the emotions of joy, contentment, and gratitude that come from this abundance. By regularly practicing this visualization exercise, we program our minds to expect and attract abundance into our lives.

In addition to reframing our thoughts and visualization, it is essential to take inspired action toward our goals. Action is the bridge between our visions of abundance and their manifestation in reality. We must take deliberate steps towards what we desire, trusting that the abundance we seek is already available to us. By aligning our thoughts, emotions, and actions with the belief in limitless possibilities, we create a powerful force that propels us toward abundance.

It is also important to cultivate a sense of worthiness and deservingness. Recognize that you are inherently deserving of the blessings and abundance that life has to offer. Release any lingering self-doubt or feelings of unworthiness, and embrace the belief that you are worthy of love, success, and abundance. By embracing your worthiness and self-value, you attract opportunities and experiences that reflect this belief.

Surrounding ourselves with uplifting and supportive individuals is another vital aspect of cultivating an abundance mindset. Seek out like-minded individuals who share your desire for growth and abundance. Engage in conversations and activities that inspire you and push you to expand your horizons. Surrounding ourselves with a positive and supportive community helps to reinforce our belief in abundance and reminds us that we are not alone on this journey.

Finally, be patient and trust in the process. Shifting from a scarcity mindset to an abundance mindset is a journey that requires time, dedication, and self-reflection. There may be moments of doubt or setbacks along the way, but remember that obstacles are merely opportunities for growth. Trust that the universe is conspiring in your favor and that abundance is your birthright.

As we conclude this chapter on recognizing and overcoming the scarcity mindset, take a moment to reflect on the insights and strategies shared. Recognize that your journey toward an abundance mindset is unique and personal. Embrace the power of gratitude, visualization, action, worthiness, and supportive communities as you cultivate an abundant mindset. Trust that by actively practicing and embodying these principles, you are aligning yourself with the limitless possibilities that abundance offers.

Remember, mastering the art of instantaneous gratitude for a wealthy mindset is a continuous practice. Embrace this transformative journey and know that with every step, you are expanding your capacity to receive and attract abundance. The next chapter will explore how cultivating a mindset of gratitude further opens the doors to abundant living. Stay tuned, and continue on this remarkable path of transformation and growth.

Chapter 3: Shifting Your Perspective: From Lack to Abundance

In our journey towards abundance, one of the key steps is to shift our perspective from scarcity to abundance. It is a shift that allows us to break free from the chains of limitation and open ourselves up to a world of infinite possibilities. By mastering this art of instantaneous gratitude, we can cultivate a wealthy mindset that attracts wealth and opportunities into our lives effortlessly.

The mind is a powerful tool that shapes our reality. It is through our thoughts and beliefs that we create our experiences and attract what we desire. Unfortunately, many of us have been conditioned to believe in scarcity. We have been taught that there is not enough to go around and that we must fight tooth and nail for our share. This scarcity mindset keeps us trapped in a cycle of lack and prevents us from experiencing true abundance.

So how do we break free from this limited perspective and embrace abundance? It starts with a conscious decision to change our thoughts and beliefs. We must be willing to challenge the notion of scarcity and open ourselves up to the idea that there is more than enough for everyone. This shift in mindset is not always easy, but with practice and persistence, it becomes second nature.

One practical technique to change your mindset from scarcity to abundance is the practice of gratitude. Gratitude is a powerful force that instantly shifts our focus from what we lack to what we have. When we cultivate an attitude of gratitude, we are able to recognize and appreciate the abundance that already exists in our lives.

Begin by making a list of things you are grateful for each day. It could be as simple as a warm cup of coffee in the morning or the smile of a loved one. Take a moment to truly feel the gratitude in your heart. As you consistently practice gratitude, you will find that your perspective begins to shift. Instead of dwelling on what you don't have, you will start to see the abundance all around you.

Another technique to shift your perspective is the power of affirmations. Affirmations are positive statements that help reprogram your subconscious mind. By repeating affirmations daily, you can train your mind to focus on abundance and attract more of it into your life.

Create a list of affirmations that inspire you and resonate with your desire for abundance. Repeat them daily, either silently or out loud, and believe in the truth of these statements. Gradually, your subconscious mind will absorb these affirmations, and they will become your new reality.

Visualization is another powerful tool to shift your perspective from lack to abundance. Take a few moments each day to visualize yourself living a life of abundance. See yourself surrounded by wealth, opportunities, and success. Imagine the feeling of joy and fulfillment that comes with abundance. By consistently visualizing this reality, you are aligning yourself with the energy of abundance and attracting it into your life.

As you practice these techniques, you will begin to notice subtle shifts in your thinking and behavior. You will feel more open, optimistic, and receptive to opportunities. Doors that were once closed will start to swing open, and you will find yourself embracing abundance with open arms.

Remember, shifting from scarcity to abundance is an ongoing process. It requires dedication and persistence to rewire years of conditioning. But with each step forward, you are one step closer to mastering the art of instantaneous gratitude and cultivating a wealthy mindset.

The journey towards abundance continues in the next part of this chapter. We will explore further techniques and delve deeper into the mindset required to attract and manifest wealth. Stay tuned for the exciting second half as we unlock the secrets of abundance and empower ourselves to create a life of limitless possibilities. Now that we have explored practical techniques to shift our perspective from scarcity to abundance, let's delve even deeper into the mindset required to attract and manifest wealth. In this second half of Chapter 3, we will uncover more secrets of abundance and empower ourselves to create a life of limitless possibilities.

One crucial mindset shift on our journey towards abundance is to let go of fear and embrace trust. Often, our scarcity mindset is rooted in fear – fear of not having enough, fear of failure, fear of missing out. This fear keeps us trapped and prevents us from taking risks and seizing opportunities. To truly cultivate a wealthy mindset, we must release these fears and trust in our innate ability to create the life we desire.

To let go of fear, it is essential to develop a strong sense of self-worth and self-belief. Understand that you are worthy of abundance and success, just as much as anyone else. Remind yourself daily of your strengths, talents, and accomplishments. Affirmations like "I am deserving of abundance" and "I am capable of attracting wealth" can reinforce this belief in your subconscious mind.

Another powerful mindset shift towards abundance is to adopt the attitude of possibility. Instead of seeing limitations and obstacles, start viewing challenges as opportunities for growth and learning. Embrace a mindset that says, "I can overcome anything that comes my way." This perspective opens doors and invites new possibilities into your life.

Additionally, surround yourself with positive people who also have an abundance mindset. Connect with individuals who inspire and support you on your journey towards wealth and success. By surrounding yourself with like-minded individuals, you create a positive and empowering environment that reinforces your goals and beliefs.

Further, when it comes to attracting wealth, it is important to understand the importance of taking inspired action. While embracing a mindset of abundance is crucial, it must be accompanied by intentional and focused action. Ask yourself, "What steps can I take today to move closer to my financial goals?" Then, take action and follow through. Remember, the universe rewards those who take aligned action towards their desires.

Additionally, practicing detachment is a key aspect of the abundance mindset. This does not mean being indifferent or giving up on your goals. Instead, it means releasing your attachment to specific outcomes and trusting that the universe will provide in the best possible way. By letting go of control and surrendering to the flow of abundance, you allow space for miraculous manifestations to occur.

Another technique to shift your mindset from lack to abundance is to develop a habit of generosity. Cultivate the belief that there is enough abundance in the world for everyone, including yourself. Actively seek opportunities to give and contribute, whether through acts of kindness, donating to causes you care about, or sharing your knowledge and skills with others. The more you give, the more abundance you attract into your life.

Finally, celebrate and acknowledge your progress along the way. Recognize and appreciate the small wins and achievements on your journey towards abundance. By celebrating every step forward, you reinforce a positive mindset and attract more positive experiences into your life.

As we reach the end of this chapter, remember that shifting from scarcity to abundance is a lifelong journey. It requires consistent effort and commitment to nurture and strengthen our wealthy mindset. However, each step forward brings us closer to a life of unlimited possibilities and abundance.

In the next chapter, we will explore strategies for aligning our actions and behaviors with our wealth mindset. We will uncover how habits, routines, and intentional choices can accelerate our journey towards financial abundance. Get ready to dive deeper into the practical aspects of mastering the art of instantaneous gratitude and embracing a wealthy mindset.

Thank you for joining me on this transformative journey. May your path towards abundance be filled with joy, growth, and endless opportunities.

Chapter 4: Mastering Instantaneous Gratitude

Have you ever experienced a moment when everything seemed to fall into place? A moment when you felt an overwhelming sense of joy and appreciation for the simplest things in life? This is the power of instantaneous gratitude.

In our fast-paced world, it's easy to get caught up in the hustle and bustle of daily life. We often find ourselves chasing after bigger and better things, constantly striving for more. But amidst this pursuit of abundance, we often overlook the abundance that already surrounds us.

Instantaneous gratitude is about recognizing and appreciating the goodness in our lives in real-time. It's about shifting our focus from scarcity to abundance, and embracing a wealthy mindset that fosters contentment and fulfillment. By mastering this art, we can transform our entire perspective on life.

So how do we unlock the secrets to experiencing instantaneous gratitude? It begins with cultivating awareness. Life moves at a rapid pace, and if we're not intentional, we can easily miss the little moments of joy and beauty that are peppered throughout our days.

Start by setting aside a few moments each day to simply be still and observe. Take in the sights, sounds, and sensations around you. Notice the intricate details of nature, the warmth of the sun on your skin, or the laughter of a loved one. By truly immersing ourselves in the present moment, we open ourselves up to a deeper sense of gratitude.

Another powerful tool for mastering instantaneous gratitude is practicing mindfulness. Mindfulness is about being fully present and engaged in the current moment, without judgment or attachment to the past or future. It allows us to appreciate the richness of each experience as it unfolds.

One effective way to cultivate mindfulness is through a gratitude journal. Take a few minutes each day to reflect on the things you're grateful for. Write them down, savoring each blessing and acknowledging the positive impact it has had on your life. As you engage in this practice, you'll develop a heightened sense of appreciation and an increased ability to recognize the abundance that surrounds you.

But mastering instantaneous gratitude goes beyond individual practices; it's about cultivating an attitude of gratitude in all aspects of life. It involves shifting our perspective from what we lack to what we already have. By focusing on the positives, we invite more positivity into our lives.

One way to nurture this mindset is by expressing gratitude to others. Take a moment to acknowledge and thank those who have made a difference in your life. Whether it's a family member, friend, or even a stranger, expressing gratitude not only strengthens relationships but also enhances our own sense of happiness and fulfillment.

Gratitude can also be channeled into acts of kindness. By extending a helping hand to those in need, we not only make a positive impact on their lives but also deepen our gratitude for the blessings we possess. Small acts of kindness can lead to a ripple effect, spreading positivity and gratitude throughout the world.

As you embark on your journey to mastering instantaneous gratitude, remember that it's a practice. It takes time and consistency to shift our mindset and fully embrace this transformative way of living. But with each moment of awareness, each expression of gratitude, we come one step closer to experiencing true abundance.

By cultivating mindfulness, expressing gratitude, and embracing the little moments of joy, we can transform our lives from scarcity to abundance. The power to unlock limitless gratitude lies within each of us. So, take a deep breath, open your heart, and step into a world where abundance is everywhere you look.

*Chapter stops at the end of a sentence*As we continue our exploration of mastering instantaneous gratitude, we will delve deeper into the practices that can help us cultivate this transformative mindset in our daily lives. So, grab a cup of tea, find a cozy spot, and let's continue our journey towards abundant living.

One powerful practice for cultivating instantaneous gratitude is the act of savoring. Savoring involves intentionally pausing to fully enjoy and appreciate the positive experiences in our lives. It's about relishing the taste of a delicious meal, cherishing a heartfelt conversation with a loved one, or basking in the beauty of a breathtaking sunset.

To savor moments, pay attention to your senses. Engage all your senses and notice the details that make the experience enjoyable. Feel the texture of the food on your tongue, delight in the aromas that waft through the air, and truly listen to the sounds surrounding you. By fully immersing ourselves in the present moment, we enhance our ability to experience gratitude and find joy in the simplest of things.

Another practice that can further enhance our ability to experience instantaneous gratitude is the intention of giving and receiving. When we intentionally give to others, not only do we sow seeds of kindness and generosity, but we also open ourselves up to receiving the abundance that flows back to us.

Acts of giving can be as simple as offering a helping hand to a stranger, donating to a charitable cause, or sharing our time and expertise with someone in need. When we give without expectation, from a place of genuine care and compassion, we invite gratitude and abundance to flow into our lives.

Equally important is our willingness to receive. Many of us find it challenging to accept help or compliments graciously. We may feel unworthy or uncomfortable being on the receiving end of generosity. But by being open to receiving, we allow others to experience the joy of giving and create a harmonious cycle of gratitude and abundance.

Additionally, incorporating rituals into our daily lives can help us cultivate instantaneous gratitude. Rituals are symbolic actions that hold deep meaning and significance for us. They provide a sense of structure and stability, grounding us in the present moment and reminding us of the abundance that surrounds us.

Rituals can take various forms, such as practicing gratitude before meals, setting intentions at the start of each day, or engaging in a gratitude meditation before bedtime. By infusing our daily routines with intentional moments of gratitude, we create a positive framework for experiencing abundance in all areas of our lives.

Lastly, it's essential to surround ourselves with people who support our journey towards mastering instantaneous gratitude. Connecting with like-minded individuals who share our values and aspirations can amplify our gratitude practice and provide a supportive community to lean on.

Seek out relationships that nurture your growth and inspire you to embrace gratitude. Join gratitude circles, participate in online communities, or attend workshops and retreats to deepen your understanding and practice of gratitude. Together, we can uplift and empower one another on this transformative path.

As we conclude this chapter on mastering instantaneous gratitude, remember that gratitude is a way of being—a constant choice we make to focus on the abundance that exists within and around us. It may take time to shift our mindset and fully embrace this way of living, but the journey itself is a beautiful and worthwhile endeavor.

By cultivating awareness, practicing mindfulness, embracing the little moments of joy, savoring experiences, giving and receiving with intention, incorporating rituals, and surrounding ourselves with a supportive community, we can gradually transform our lives from a scarcity mindset to an abundant one.

So, my friend, take a moment to appreciate how far you've come. You now hold the key to unlocking limitless gratitude and experiencing the rich tapestry of life with a wealthy mindset. Embrace each day with open arms, knowing that abundance and gratitude are always within reach.

As we bid farewell to this chapter, I leave you with these words: Gratitude is not a destination but a journey—a lifelong practice that brings us closer to the abundant blessings that await us. So go forth, my fellow traveler, and continue to cultivate instantaneous gratitude in every moment and every breath.

Remember, abundance is everywhere you look.

Chapter 5: Embracing Change for Abundance

Change. It's a word that often evokes fear and discomfort for many of us. We tend to prefer the familiar, the routine, and the predictable. But what if I told you that change is not something to be feared, but rather, a powerful tool for growth and abundance? What if I told you that by embracing change, you can adapt and thrive in any situation? Let's explore the art of embracing change and uncover the wealth of opportunities it presents.

Life is constantly changing, whether we like it or not. From the moment we are born, we are thrust into an ever-evolving world. Our circumstances, relationships, and even our own selves undergo constant shifts. It is in our best interest to understand that change is an inherent part of life's journey and that resisting it only hinders our progress towards abundance.

One of the key factors in embracing change is developing a mindset of flexibility and adaptability. When we cling too tightly to our old ways, we limit our potential for growth. It's like trying to hold on to a twig in a flowing river – the more we resist, the more it slips through our fingers. Instead, allow yourself to surrender to the forces of change, trusting that they will guide you towards greater abundance.

Embracing change also requires us to let go of our fear of the unknown. It's natural to feel anxious about what lies ahead when faced with uncertainty. However, it is through the unknown that we often discover our greatest opportunities. By shifting our perspective and seeing change as a gateway to new possibilities, we open ourselves up to a world of abundance waiting to be explored.

Change can be uncomfortable, no doubt about it. It disrupts our routines, challenges our beliefs, and pushes us out of our comfort zones. But it is within these discomfort zones that we find unprecedented growth and transformation. Think about the butterfly – it goes through a complete metamorphosis, breaking free from its old confines to emerge as a stunning creature. In the same way, change allows us to shed our old selves and step into the fullness of who we are meant to be.

As we navigate the ever-changing landscape of life, it is essential to cultivate resilience. Change brings both ups and downs, victories and setbacks. It is how we respond to these fluctuations that determines our ability to thrive. Remember, setbacks are not failures, but rather, stepping stones towards success. Learn from your experiences, adapt to the challenges, and use them to propel yourself forward.

To embrace change fully, it is crucial to cultivate a growth mindset. This mindset acknowledges that our talents and abilities can be developed through dedication and hard work. It recognizes that setbacks are not permanent but rather opportunities for learning and improvement. When faced with change, ask yourself, "How can I grow from this? What can I learn? How can I use this as a stepping stone towards abundance?"

In this rapidly changing world, the ability to embrace change is not only beneficial but necessary for our personal and professional growth. Those who resist change find themselves left behind, clinging to outdated practices and beliefs. On the other hand, those who willingly adapt and evolve are the ones who thrive. They seize the opportunities change presents and harness them to create a life of abundance.

So, I urge you to let go of your fear of change. Embrace it as a powerful tool for growth and abundance. Nurture a mindset of flexibility, resilience, and growth. As we delve deeper into this chapter, we will uncover practical strategies and insights to help you navigate the winds of change and harness their transformative power.

Remember, change is not the enemy; it is your secret ally on the path to abundance. Now, let's explore how you can unlock its potential and embark on a journey towards a wealthy mindset. Stay curious, stay open, and get ready to embrace change like never before.

Overcoming the fear and discomfort associated with change is an essential step towards embracing abundance and a wealthy mindset. In the first half of this chapter, we explored the importance of flexibility, resilience, and growth mindset in navigating the ever-changing landscape of life. Now, let's continue our journey and uncover practical strategies and insights to help you harness the transformative power of change.

One of the most effective ways to embrace change is to cultivate a sense of curiosity and openness. Instead of approaching change with apprehension, view it as an opportunity for exploration and growth. Ask yourself, "What can I learn from this situation? How can I use it to expand my horizons?" When you approach change with curiosity, you open yourself up to new perspectives and possibilities. You allow yourself to see beyond the surface and discover hidden treasures within the challenges that come your way.

Another key aspect of embracing change is developing the ability to adapt and pivot. As the famous saying goes, "The only constant in life is change." To thrive in an ever-changing world, we must learn to adapt our strategies, perspectives, and behaviors accordingly. Resist the urge to cling onto old habits and routines that no longer serve you. Instead, be willing to let go and embrace new ways of thinking and doing things. Remember, change often brings with it a wealth of opportunities that can lead to personal and professional growth.

Alongside adaptability, it is crucial to cultivate a sense of self-awareness. Take the time to reflect on your strengths, weaknesses, triggers, and emotions when faced with change. Understanding how you respond to change will enable you to better navigate through it. If you find yourself resisting or feeling overwhelmed, take a step back and examine your mindset. Are you holding onto limiting beliefs or fears? Are you operating from a scarcity mindset? By acknowledging and addressing these underlying factors, you can shift your perspective and approach change with a more positive and empowered mindset.

During times of change, it is also important to seek support and surround yourself with a network of like-minded individuals. Connecting with others who are on a similar journey allows you to share experiences, gain insights, and draw strength from one another. Additionally, seeking guidance from mentors or coaches can provide you with tools and strategies to navigate change more effectively. Remember, you don't have to go through this journey alone. Together, we can support each other in embracing change and creating a life of abundance.

As we navigate the second half of this chapter, I encourage you to take a moment for self-reflection. Consider the changes that you have resisted in the past and the impact it had on your personal growth. Identify any limiting beliefs or fears that may be holding you back from embracing change fully. What steps can you take to shift your mindset and approach change with a sense of excitement and possibility?

In conclusion, change is a powerful tool for growth and abundance. By embracing change, developing flexibility and adaptability, cultivating curiosity and self-awareness, seeking support, and shifting your mindset, you can harness the transformative power of change in your life. Remember, change is not the enemy but your secret ally on the path to abundance. Now, armed with these insights and strategies, go forth and embrace change like never before. The journey towards a wealthy mindset awaits you.

Chapter 6: Gratitude Journaling: Unleashing the Power of Writing

Have you ever stopped to truly appreciate the little blessings in your life? Those moments that often go unnoticed but have the power to bring immense joy and gratitude to our hearts. It's easy to get caught up in the hectic nature of our daily lives, constantly chasing after the next big thing. But what if I told you that you hold the key to transforming your mindset towards abundance through a simple, yet powerful practice? That's where gratitude journaling comes in.

Keeping a gratitude journal is like having a personal portal that allows you to enter a realm of positivity and abundance. It is a tangible way to shift your focus from scarcity to abundance. By making a conscious effort to record and reflect on the things you are grateful for, you invite more of those blessings into your life.

So, what exactly is gratitude journaling and how does it work? Simply put, it involves writing down things you are grateful for on a regular basis. Whether it's the presence of loved ones, a beautiful sunset, or an act of kindness, every little thing counts. The idea is to cultivate a habit of acknowledging and appreciating the abundance that surrounds you.

But the benefits of gratitude journaling go beyond a mere act of writing. It has a profound impact on your mindset, rewiring your brain to focus on the positive aspects of life. When you consistently practice gratitude and train your mind to look for the good, you become more resilient, optimistic, and open to opportunities.

One of the key benefits of gratitude journaling is its ability to shift your perspective. In a world that often emphasizes what we lack, it's easy to fall into the trap of scarcity thinking. We constantly compare ourselves to others and focus on what we don't have. However, by redirecting our attention to the blessings we do have, we start to realize just how abundant our lives truly are.

Gratitude journaling also helps us develop a deeper sense of appreciation. When we take the time to reflect on the positive experiences and people in our lives, we begin to cherish them even more. This heightened sense of appreciation paves the way for increased joy and contentment.

Moreover, the act of writing in a gratitude journal allows us to savor the positive emotions associated with gratitude. As we put pen to paper, we relive those moments of joy, love, and gratitude, amplifying their impact on our well-being. It's like capturing the essence of pleasant experiences and immortalizing them in our journal.

Another incredible aspect of gratitude journaling is its ability to bring forth a sense of abundance and attract more of it into our lives. As we focus on what we are grateful for, we naturally draw more positive experiences, people, and opportunities towards us. It's as if the universe responds to our positive energy, consistently providing us with abundance.

In the next part of this chapter, we will delve deeper into the strategies and techniques to maximize the potential of gratitude journaling. We will explore specific prompts, tips for consistency, and ways to overcome challenges that may arise along the way. By harnessing the power of writing and gratitude, you will unlock a wealth of abundance in your life.

So, grab a pen and a journal, and get ready to embark on a transformative journey. Through the practice of gratitude journaling, you will cultivate a mindset of abundance, attract positivity, and unlock the true power of instant gratitude for a wealthy mindset.

As you embark on the transformative journey of gratitude journaling, you will discover that the power of writing goes beyond simply listing the things you are grateful for. In the second half of this chapter, we will delve deeper into the strategies and techniques to maximize the potential of gratitude journaling. So, grab a pen and a journal, and let's continue unlocking the true power of gratitude for a wealthy mindset.

One powerful technique to enhance your gratitude journaling practice is to use specific prompts. These prompts can help you dig deeper and explore different aspects of your life that you may not have considered before. For example, you can start by writing about the people you are grateful for and why they bring joy to your life. Reflecting on the impact they have on you will strengthen your relationships and increase your appreciation for their presence.

Another effective prompt is to write about the challenges or hardships you have faced and find a way to extract gratitude from those experiences. This exercise can be particularly transformative as it shifts your focus from the negative aspects of those challenges to the lessons learned and personal growth they have brought about.

In addition to prompts, consistency is key in ensuring the effectiveness of your gratitude journaling practice. Set aside a specific time each day or week to write in your journal. By making it a regular habit, you train your mind to actively seek out things to be grateful for throughout the day. It may be helpful to find a quiet and peaceful space where you can fully immerse yourself in the process, allowing gratitude to flow effortlessly onto the pages of your journal.

While consistency is important, it's also essential to approach gratitude journaling with a sense of playfulness and exploration. Allow your creativity to shine through by incorporating colors, drawings, or even photographs into your journal. Create a visual representation of the abundance in your life and let it serve as a reminder of the blessings that surround you.

Of course, like any practice, gratitude journaling may present challenges along the way. There may be days when you feel uninspired or overwhelmed, making it difficult to find words to express your gratitude. In these moments, it can be helpful to look for inspiration outside of yourself. Seek out gratitude quotes or stories that resonate with you and use them as a starting point for your journal entry. Remember, the act of searching for gratitude can often reignite the flame of appreciation within you.

It's also important to keep in mind that gratitude journaling is not a competition or a race. It's about your personal growth and self-discovery. Do not compare your journal or your journey to others. Embrace your own unique path and celebrate the progress you make along the way. Every entry, no matter how big or small, is a step towards cultivating an abundant mindset.

As you continue on this journey of gratitude journaling, you will notice an incredible shift in your mindset. The more you focus on gratitude, the more abundance you attract into your life. Opportunities will unfold, relationships will deepen, and joy will become a constant companion on your path.

By harnessing the power of writing and gratitude, you have the ability to transform your mindset from a place of scarcity to a state of abundance. Allow your gratitude journal to serve as a portal to this realm of limitless possibilities. Embrace the practice with an open heart and an open mind, and watch as your entire life begins to radiate with the energy of gratitude.

Congratulations on completing the second half of this chapter! May your journey of gratitude journaling continue to bring you immense joy, abundance, and a truly wealthy mindset.

Chapter 7: The Abundance Mindset in Relationships

When we think of abundance, our minds often drift to thoughts of financial wealth and material possessions. However, the abundance mindset goes beyond monetary gains and extends into every aspect of our lives, including relationships. We often underestimate the power of cultivating an abundance mindset in building healthy, fulfilling connections with others.

At its core, the abundance mindset in relationships is centered around the belief that there is enough love, support, and happiness to go around for everyone. It encourages us to release feelings of scarcity, competition, and jealousy, and instead embrace a mindset of gratitude and appreciation for the connections we have. By adopting this mindset, we open ourselves up to experiencing deeper and more meaningful relationships, both personally and professionally.

In our personal lives, the abundance mindset allows us to approach our relationships with curiosity and an open heart. It teaches us to celebrate the successes and happiness of our loved ones, rather than feeling threatened or envious. When we genuinely rejoice in the joy and achievements of those close to us, it creates an environment of love, trust, and support. We begin to realize that their accomplishments do not diminish our own, but rather inspire us to reach for our own greatness.

Moreover, the abundance mindset teaches us to embrace vulnerability in our relationships. Instead of fearing rejection or betrayal, we choose to believe that there is an abundance of love and kindness to be shared. This allows us to take risks, express our true selves, and deepen our emotional connections. When we approach relationships with an open and vulnerable heart, we create a space for authentic and meaningful connections to flourish.

In addition to personal relationships, the abundance mindset has a profound impact on our professional interactions as well. When we view the professional world through the lens of abundance, we shift our mindset from one of competition to collaboration. We understand that there are endless opportunities for success, growth, and fulfillment in our careers. Rather than being threatened by the achievements of our colleagues, we see them as potential mentors, collaborators, and inspirations.

With an abundance mindset, we approach networking and building professional relationships with genuine interest and curiosity rather than a transactional mindset. We seek to support and uplift others, recognizing that their success does not diminish our own. By fostering a spirit of collaboration and abundance, we create a professional network that is rooted in connection, trust, and collective growth.

Cultivating an abundance mindset in relationships requires a conscious effort and practice. It requires us to shift our mindset, challenge our limiting beliefs, and reframe our perspectives. But the rewards are immeasurable. As we embrace the abundance mindset, we open ourselves up to a world of possibilities – a world where our relationships are nourishing, uplifting, and transformative.

So, as we navigate the complexities of personal and professional relationships, let us remember the power of the abundance mindset. As we release scarcity and embrace gratitude, we create a space for love, connection, and growth to thrive. Stay tuned for the second half of this chapter, where we will dive deeper into practical strategies to cultivate an abundance mindset in relationships. Get ready to unlock the true potential of your connections, both personal and professional. There is so much more to explore!

And with that, we leave you, eager and excited to continue this journey with you. The adventure awaits, and the possibilities are endless. The Abundance Mindset in Relationships (continued)

Now that we have explored the power of cultivating an abundance mindset in relationships, let's dive deeper into practical strategies to help you embrace this mindset in your personal and professional connections.

One of the first steps in cultivating an abundance mindset is practicing gratitude. Take a moment to reflect on the relationships in your life and identify aspects that you are genuinely grateful for. It could be the love and support of your family, the friendships that bring joy and laughter, or the professional connections that have opened doors of opportunity. By acknowledging and appreciating these blessings, you shift your focus from scarcity to abundance.

Expressing gratitude to those who contribute to your relationships is equally important. Whether it's a simple "thank you" or a heartfelt note, expressing gratitude reinforces the abundance mindset and strengthens the bond you share. It creates a ripple effect, inspiring others to embrace their own abundance mindset and fostering a culture of appreciation and support.

Another practical way to cultivate an abundance mindset is through conscious acts of kindness. Look for opportunities to be generous and supportive in your relationships. It could be offering a listening ear to a friend in need, volunteering your time for a cause you believe in, or sharing your expertise to help a colleague grow. These acts of kindness not only nourish your relationships but also reinforce the belief that there is enough goodness to go around for everyone.

Moreover, embracing empathy and understanding is essential in cultivating an abundance mindset in relationships. Take the time to understand the perspectives and experiences of others. Practice active listening and engage in meaningful conversations that foster connection. By genuinely seeking to understand, you create a safe space for your loved ones and colleagues to share their thoughts, dreams, and challenges without judgment.

In addition to these strategies, setting healthy boundaries is crucial for sustaining an abundance mindset in relationships. Boundaries help maintain a balance between giving and receiving, ensuring that you are nurturing yourself while also supporting others. They empower you to make choices that align with your values, priorities, and overall well-being. Remember, saying "no" when necessary is an act of self-care and self-respect.

Lastly, let go of comparison and embrace your authentic self. It's easy to fall into the trap of comparing ourselves to others, but it only reinforces feelings of scarcity and inadequacy. Instead, celebrate your unique strengths and accomplishments. Recognize that your journey is different from anyone else's, and that's what makes it special. When you embrace your true self and celebrate your own growth, you inspire others to do the same.

As we wrap up this chapter, I invite you to reflect on your own relationships—both personal and professional. How can you incorporate these strategies to create a more abundant mindset? Remember, fruitful relationships come from a place of abundance, where love, support, and happiness are abundant for all.

The adventure of cultivating an abundance mindset in relationships is ongoing. It requires practice, patience, and a willingness to continue growing. But as you embrace this mindset, you will uncover the transformative power it holds.

So, go forth with renewed purpose and confidence. Embrace the abundance mindset in your relationships, and watch as love, connection, and growth flourish. You have the power to create a world where abundance is the norm. It starts with you and extends to all those you encounter.

Thank you for joining us on this journey of mastering the art of instantaneous gratitude for a wealthy mindset. Stay tuned for future explorations into other aspects of abundance and self-growth. Remember, there is no limit to what you can achieve when you choose abundance.

Keep nurturing your relationships, keep fostering gratitude, and keep embracing the abundance mindset. The rewards will be extraordinary.

Chapter 8: Overcoming Limiting Beliefs

Uncover the root causes of your limiting beliefs and acquire effective strategies to break free from their constraints.

Limiting beliefs are like invisible chains that hold us back from achieving our true potential. They are deeply ingrained thoughts and perceptions that restrict us, keeping us from reaching our goals and living a fulfilling life. These beliefs often stem from childhood experiences, societal conditioning, or past failures, and they can create strong mental barriers that hinder our progress.

But here's the good news: limiting beliefs are not permanent. With awareness and the right strategies, we can overcome them and create empowering beliefs that propel us towards abundance. In this chapter, we'll delve into the profound process of uncovering the root causes of your limiting beliefs and equipping yourself with effective tools to break free from their grip.

To begin this transformative journey, it is crucial to develop self-awareness. Pause for a moment and reflect on a belief that currently holds you back. It could be a belief about your abilities, worthiness, or the limitations of your circumstances. By identifying and acknowledging these beliefs, you take the first step towards dismantling their influence over your life.

Once you've pinpointed a specific limiting belief, it's time to explore its origins. Often, these beliefs are firmly grounded in our past experiences. Ask yourself: Where did this belief come from? Was it shaped by a significant event or interaction? Understanding the root cause helps illuminate the triggers that perpetuate the belief, allowing you to challenge its validity.

As you embark on this introspective journey, remember to approach yourself with compassion and non-judgment. Acknowledge that these beliefs were formed as a means of protection or adaptation in certain situations. By extending empathy towards yourself, you create an environment conducive to growth and transformation.

With a deeper understanding of the origins of your limiting beliefs, you can start to challenge their validity. Begin by examining the evidence that supports or counters these beliefs. Are there instances where you've proven them wrong? Are there alternative perspectives that challenge this belief?

Engage in a process of questioning and critical thinking. Ask yourself: What if this belief is not true? How would my life change if I let go of this belief? By challenging the assumptions underlying your limiting beliefs, you open up the possibility for new, empowering beliefs to emerge.

Now, let's explore a powerful strategy to break free from the constraints of limiting beliefs: reframing. Reframing involves consciously shifting your perspective to create a more empowering interpretation of a situation or belief.

Imagine a scenario where you believe you are not smart enough to succeed in a particular field. Instead of accepting this belief as an absolute truth, try reframing it. Focus on your strengths, past achievements, and the skills you possess that could contribute to success in that field. By reframing your belief, you open the door to new possibilities and pave the way for personal growth.

In addition to reframing, another effective strategy to overcome limiting beliefs is visualization. Visualization allows you to vividly imagine yourself taking action, succeeding, and rewriting your narrative. By consistently visualizing positive outcomes, you program your mind to shed the limitations of your previous beliefs and embrace new, empowering ones.

As you conclude this first half of the chapter, pause and reflect on the insights gained so far. You've explored the origins of your limiting beliefs, challenged their validity, and discovered powerful strategies to liberate yourself from their constraints. But there's more to come in the second half of this chapter. So, brace yourself for the surprising revelations and transformative exercises that lie ahead.

Remember, your journey towards overcoming limiting beliefs is an ongoing process. Embrace curiosity, resilience, and the willingness to question your beliefs. As you continue developing a mindset of abundance and release the shackles of scarcity, a world of infinite possibilities awaits you. Stay tuned for the next part of this chapter, where we dive even deeper into the transformative realm of overcoming limiting beliefs. Now that you have delved into the origins of your limiting beliefs and equipped yourself with powerful strategies for overcoming them, it's time to deepen your transformation and unlock the full potential of your abundant mindset. In the second half of this chapter, we will explore further techniques and exercises that will aid you on your journey to a wealthy mindset.

One effective strategy to overcome limiting beliefs is the practice of affirmations. Affirmations are positive statements that you repeat to yourself on a regular basis, reaffirming new empowering beliefs. By consistently affirming what you desire and countering your limiting beliefs, you are reprogramming your subconscious mind to embrace abundance and success. For example, if you have a belief that you are not worthy of financial abundance, you can create an affirmation such as "I am worthy of infinite wealth and abundance in all areas of my life."

To enhance the effectiveness of affirmations, it is important to engage your senses and emotions while repeating them. Visualize yourself already embodying the belief you desire, feel the emotions associated with it, and truly embody the essence of your desired state.

Repeat your affirmations daily, ideally in front of a mirror, and watch as your mindset shifts towards prosperity.

Another powerful technique to overcome limiting beliefs is the practice of gratitude. Gratitude is a key element in cultivating an abundant mindset as it shifts your focus from scarcity to abundance. Take a moment each day to reflect on the things you are grateful for, whether big or small. By consciously acknowledging and appreciating the blessings in your life, you are rewiring your brain to focus on the positive aspects, creating a magnet for more abundance and success.

In addition to gratitude, visualization can further amplify your journey towards overcoming limiting beliefs. Visualization is a process of mentally picturing and experiencing your desired outcomes. Take some time each day to create vivid mental images of yourself already living the life you desire. Imagine every detail, engage your senses, and allow yourself to feel the emotions associated with achieving your goals. This powerful practice helps to reprogram your subconscious mind and align it with your conscious desires, paving the way for success.

To complement these techniques, it is essential to surround yourself with a supportive environment that encourages growth and empowerment. Seek out like-minded individuals who share similar goals and aspirations, and engage in meaningful conversations that uplift and inspire you. Connect with mentors or coaches who can guide you on your journey, and participate in personal development workshops or courses. Surrounding yourself with positivity and motivation will fuel your progress and reinforce your beliefs in your ability to achieve greatness.

As you continue on your path towards a wealthy mindset, remember to be patient and kind to yourself. Transforming limiting beliefs requires time and consistent effort. Embrace every small victory along the way, knowing that each step forward brings you closer to your desired state of abundance.

In conclusion, you have embarked on a powerful journey of overcoming limiting beliefs. By uncovering their roots, questioning their validity, and implementing effective strategies, you are well on your way to realizing your true potential. Affirmations, gratitude, visualization, and a supportive environment will further propel you towards success. Keep the conversation with yourself and others focused on empowerment and growth. Trust the process, stay committed, and watch as your mindset expands, leading you to a life of abundance and fulfillment.

Congratulations on completing this chapter! Remember, this journey of transforming limiting beliefs is just the beginning. Stay tuned for the next chapter, where we will delve into the realm of abundance manifestation and explore the art of attracting wealth and prosperity into your life.

Chapter 9: Manifesting Abundance: The Law of Attraction

Every day, we are bombarded with thoughts, beliefs, and external factors that deeply shape our perception of scarcity. We often find ourselves trapped in a mindset that focuses on lack and limitation, unaware of the tremendous power we have within us to manifest abundance. But what if I told you that you possess the key to unlock a world of infinite possibilities? What if I revealed to you the secret force that can bring forth everything you desire? Welcome to the transformative power of the Law of Attraction.

The Law of Attraction is a universal principle that states that like attracts like. In other words, the energy you emit into the universe will attract similar energy back into your life. This means that if you constantly think negative thoughts and believe in scarcity, you will continue to attract experiences and circumstances that align with those frequencies. However, when you shift your focus to positive and abundant thoughts, the Law of Attraction will respond accordingly, bringing prosperity and abundance into your reality.

To harness the power of the Law of Attraction, it is essential to understand that your thoughts and emotions are like magnets, constantly sending out energetic signals to the universe. These signals act like a cosmic order form, telling the universe what you desire and drawing it towards you. The key lies in mastering your mindset and aligning your thoughts, emotions, and actions with the abundance you seek.

One of the most powerful techniques to manifest abundance through the Law of Attraction is visualization. Close your eyes and vividly imagine the life you want to create. See yourself living it, feeling the joy, success, and fulfillment that comes with it. By immersing yourself in the experience of abundance, you align your energy with that of your desires, sending out a clear signal to the universe.

Another essential aspect of manifesting abundance is gratitude. Gratitude acts as a powerful magnet, attracting more of what you are grateful for into your life. Take a moment each day to cultivate a practice of gratitude. Reflect on all the blessings, big and small, that surround you. By acknowledging and appreciating the abundance already present in your life, you create a positive vibration that attracts even more abundance.

It is important to recognize that the Law of Attraction operates beyond just thoughts and emotions. Your actions play a fundamental role in the manifestation process. Take inspired action towards your goals and dreams. Step outside your comfort zone and seize opportunities that align with your vision of abundance. The universe responds to your determination and commitment, guiding you towards the path of success.

Remember, the Law of Attraction is not a quick fix or a magical solution. It requires patience, consistency, and unwavering belief in the power of abundance. Embrace the journey and be open to the infinite possibilities that can unfold when you align your energy with the frequencies of prosperity.

As we delve deeper into the art of manifesting abundance through the Law of Attraction, we will explore specific techniques, exercises, and examples that will empower you to consciously create a wealthy mindset. Unlocking the unlimited potential within you is a transformative journey, and with each step, you will inch closer to a life filled with abundance.

Stay tuned for the second half of this chapter, where we delve further into the practical application of the Law of Attraction for manifesting abundance in all areas of your life. Prepare to be amazed by the power that resides within you to shape your reality. The path to abundance awaits you, and the universe is conspiring in your favor. As we continue our exploration of manifesting abundance through the Law of Attraction, let's delve further into practical techniques and exercises that will empower you to consciously create a wealthy mindset. Prepare to be amazed by the power that resides within you to shape your reality.

One powerful technique to harness the Law of Attraction is the use of affirmations. Affirmations are positive statements that reinforce your beliefs and help to reprogram your subconscious mind. By consistently repeating affirmations that align with the abundance you desire, you are signaling to the universe your intention to attract prosperity.

For example, you might say, "I am deserving of all the abundance that flows into my life," or "I attract wealth and success effortlessly." These affirmations help to shift your mindset from one of scarcity to one of abundance, allowing you to tap into the infinite possibilities that surround you.

To maximize the effectiveness of affirmations, it's important to state them in the present tense, as if they are already true. Feel the emotions associated with your desires as you affirm them, as though they are already manifesting in your life. This emotional connection strengthens the vibrational frequency you are emitting and amplifies its attraction power.

In addition to affirmations, another powerful tool for manifesting abundance is the practice of scripting. Scripting involves writing down your desires and experiences as if they have already happened. By vividly describing the life you desire, you are imprinting your intentions into your subconscious mind and sending a clear message to the universe.

Let your imagination run wild as you script your ideal life. Write about your dream job, your dream home, your ideal relationships, and all the experiences that bring you joy and fulfillment. As you read and reread your script, immerse yourself in the emotions and sensations associated with living in abundance. This process reinforces your belief in the unlimited possibilities available to you and strengthens your ability to manifest your desires.

Another powerful practice is the use of vision boards. A vision board is a visual representation of your dreams and desires. It can be a physical board where you cut out and paste images, words, and phrases that represent what you want to manifest. Alternatively, you can create a digital vision board using online tools or apps.

The key to a successful vision board is to select images and words that evoke a strong emotional response within you. Look for pictures that make you feel excited, inspired, and grateful for what you are attracting into your life. Place your vision board somewhere you can see it daily, and spend a few moments each day visualizing yourself already living the life you desire.

Finally, it is essential to cultivate an unwavering belief in the power of abundance. Doubt and skepticism can block the flow of positive energy and hinder your ability to manifest your desires. Trust that the universe is always working in your favor and that you deserve to live a life of abundance in all areas.

Surround yourself with positive influences and connect with individuals who share your belief in the power of manifestation. Seek out books, podcasts, and other resources that support your journey towards a wealthy mindset. The more you immerse yourself in a positive and abundant environment, the more your beliefs and thoughts will align with your desires.

As we conclude our exploration of manifesting abundance through the Law of Attraction, remember that you are the creator of your reality. You possess the power to shape your life by consciously directing your thoughts, emotions, and actions. Trust in the process, be patient, and continue to align your energy with the frequencies of prosperity.

The path to abundance is not always easy, and there may be challenges and setbacks along the way. But remember that every obstacle is an opportunity for growth and learning. Embrace the journey, stay focused on your desires, and maintain a mindset of gratitude and abundance.

Congratulations on taking the first steps towards mastering the art of instantaneous gratitude for a wealthy mindset. By utilizing the principles of the Law of Attraction, practicing affirmations, scripting, creating vision boards, and cultivating unwavering belief, you are well on your way to manifesting abundance in all areas of your life.

Now, it is time to put these principles into action and watch as your desires unfold before your eyes. Trust in the process, believe in your ability to manifest abundance, and prepare to witness the magic that unfolds when you align your thoughts, emotions, and actions with your dreams.

The universe is conspiring in your favor, and as you continue your journey, may you discover the limitless possibilities that await you. Embrace the power of the Law of Attraction and step into a life of abundance, success, and fulfillment.

Chapter 10: Visualization for Abundance

Discover the power of visualization as a manifestation tool and how it can accelerate your progress towards an abundant mindset.

Visualization is a technique that allows us to create mental images of our desires, goals, and dreams. It involves using our imagination to vividly picture ourselves already living the life we desire, experiencing the abundance we seek. By harnessing the power of visualization, we can tap into the limitless potential of our minds and pave the way towards a wealthy mindset.

Have you ever heard the phrase "seeing is believing"? Well, when it comes to abundance, it goes much deeper than that. Visualization bridges the gap between where we are now and where we desire to be. It helps us align our thoughts, emotions, and actions with our aspirations, ultimately attracting the abundant life we envision.

So how does visualization work? The mind is a powerful tool, and by engaging in vivid mental imagery, we stimulate the creative force within ourselves. As we visualize ourselves in our desired circumstances, whether it be financial success, fulfilling relationships, or optimal health, our brain starts constructing new neural pathways. These pathways then become ingrained in our subconscious, creating a blueprint for our reality.

When we consistently engage in visualization, our minds start to recognize these mental images as actual memories. They become familiar, comfortable, and believable. This process primes our subconscious to seek opportunities and make choices that align with our vision. By vividly picturing our goals and dreams, we are instructing our minds to focus on the aspects of life that will lead us to abundance.

Visualization not only influences our thoughts and actions but also impacts our emotions. As we immerse ourselves in the experience of our desired reality, we can tap into the feelings of joy, gratitude, and fulfillment that come with it. These positive emotions act as powerful magnets, attracting more of what we desire into our lives.

One of the essential steps in effective visualization is to engage all our senses. It's not enough to create a mental image; we must also immerse ourselves in the sounds, smells, tastes, and physical sensations associated with our desires. By involving our senses, we bring our visualizations to life, enhancing the impact on our subconscious and strengthening our belief in the possibilities.

If you're new to visualization, it may take some practice to develop the skill. Start by setting aside a dedicated time each day, preferably in a quiet and peaceful environment, where you can fully immerse yourself in the experience. Close your eyes, take a deep breath, and let your imagination run wild. Imagine every detail of your desired reality, focusing on the emotions and sensations it brings forth.

Remember, consistency is key. The more frequently you engage in visualization, the more your mind will become attuned to the abundant possibilities around you. Regular practice rewires your brain and redirects your focus towards abundance, making it a natural part of your daily thoughts and actions.

Visualization is not simply daydreaming; it is an active process of consciously creating our reality. It has been used by countless successful individuals to achieve their goals, from athletes who visualize victory to entrepreneurs who manifest their business successes. By tapping into this powerful technique, we can accelerate our progress towards an abundant mindset and create the life we truly desire.

As we embark on this journey of visualization for abundance, remember that there are no limits to what you can achieve. The power lies within you, waiting to be unlocked. So, dare to dream big, visualize your desires with unwavering belief, and watch as the universe conspires to make them a reality.

Visualization is a technique that can transform your mindset and attract abundance into your life. In the previous section, we explored how visualization works and its profound impact on our thoughts, actions, and emotions. Now, let's delve deeper into the practical steps and strategies to ensure effective visualization for abundance.

To begin, it's important to create a clear and detailed mental image of your desired reality. Close your eyes, take a deep breath, and step into the vibrant world of your dreams. Visualize every aspect of your abundant life, from the luxurious house you live in to the fulfilling relationships you have. Immerse yourself in the sensations, sights, sounds, tastes, and even smells that accompany your desired reality. The more vivid and lifelike you can make your visualization, the more effective it will be.

Alongside visualizing your desired reality, it's crucial to engage your senses on a deeper level. For example, if you envision yourself traveling, imagine the feel of the soft sand between your toes as you walk on an exotic beach. Picture the serene sound of waves crashing against the shore and the refreshing scent of the ocean breeze. By involving multiple senses, you're enhancing the impact of your visualizations and reinforcing the belief that your dreams are within reach.

Consistency is key in mastering the art of visualization. Make it a daily practice, carving out dedicated time in your schedule to focus solely on visualization. Whether it's five minutes in the morning or before bed, find a time that works for you. The regularity of this practice will train your mind to align with the abundant possibilities around you, making it a natural part of your daily thoughts and actions.

While visualization is a powerful tool, it should not replace taking action towards your goals. Visualization acts as a catalyst for motivation, inspiration, and focus, but it must be accompanied by effort and perseverance. Use your visualizations as a roadmap, guiding your actions and decisions towards the abundant life you desire. Trust that opportunities will arise, and be ready to take bold steps forward when they do.

Another technique to enhance your visualization practice is to create a vision board. A vision board is a visual representation of your desired reality, consisting of images, quotes, and affirmations that resonate with your goals. It serves as a powerful visual reminder of your aspirations and keeps you constantly connected to your vision. Place your vision board somewhere you'll see it every day, allowing your subconscious mind to absorb and reinforce the images and ideas it contains.

As you continue to visualize, it's essential to cultivate an attitude of gratitude. Express thankfulness for both your current blessings and the abundant future you're manifesting. Gratitude amplifies the positive emotions associated with your visualizations and sends out a powerful energetic signal to the universe. The more you appreciate what you already have, the more you'll attract abundance into your life.

Like any skill, visualization takes practice and patience. Don't be discouraged if you find it challenging at first. Simply commit to consistent practice and trust in the process. With time, you'll notice the transformative effects on your mindset, actions, and manifestations.

Remember, you possess unlimited potential to create a life filled with abundance and joy. The power to manifest your dreams lies within you. Visualization is a pathway to unlock that power and align your thoughts, emotions, and actions with the life you desire.

As we conclude this chapter on visualization for abundance, always carry with you the unshakable belief that your dreams are possible. Embrace the art of visualization as a manifestation tool, and let it guide you towards a wealthy mindset. Dare to dream big, trust in your power to create, and watch as the universe conspires to bring your desires to fruition.

Now, take a moment to sit in stillness, visualize your abundant future, and let your dreams unfold before you. You have the ability to transform your life and live in a state of ultimate gratitude, abundance, and fulfillment. Embrace the power of visualization, unleash your potential, and know that the wealth of your dreams is just a thought away.

Chapter 11: Gratitude as a Daily Practice

As we embark on the journey of mastering the art of instantaneous gratitude for a wealthy mindset, it is essential to create a daily practice that allows us to embody gratitude fully. In this chapter, we will explore practical ways to incorporate gratitude into our daily routine, making it an integral part of our lives for lasting abundance.

In our fast-paced world, it's easy to get caught up in the chaos and overlook the beauty that surrounds us. We often find ourselves yearning for more, focusing on what we lack rather than what we have. However, by consciously practicing gratitude, we can shift our perspective and open the doors to abundance.

One powerful way to incorporate gratitude into our daily lives is through the practice of journaling. Every morning or evening, take a few moments to reflect on the things you are grateful for. Write them down in a dedicated gratitude journal, allowing yourself to dive deep into the feelings of appreciation. Whether it's a kind gesture from a stranger, a moment of laughter, or a personal accomplishment, noting these moments of gratitude amplifies their impact.

Another method to infuse gratitude into our daily routine is by incorporating a gratitude ritual. This can be as simple as expressing gratitude before meals, acknowledging the nourishment provided by our food and the efforts of those involved in its production. Taking a moment to pause and reflect on the abundance before us can create a sense of reverence and deepen our connection to gratitude.

In addition to journaling and rituals, incorporating acts of kindness into our daily lives can foster a mindset of gratitude. Small gestures, such as sending a genuine message of appreciation to a loved one or complimenting a stranger, have the power to uplift both the receiver and the giver. By spreading gratitude through acts of kindness, we create a ripple effect that extends far beyond ourselves.

Practicing gratitude also involves shifting our focus from material possessions to the intangible blessings in our lives. We often get caught up in the pursuit of acquiring wealth and possessions, forgetting that true abundance lies in our relationships, health, and personal growth. Take the time to acknowledge and appreciate the people who bring joy and support to your life. Cultivate gratitude for the lessons learned during challenging times, as they contribute to your growth and resilience.

Furthermore, integrating gratitude into our daily routine requires mindfulness and presence. Let's take a moment to pause, breathe, and observe the beauty that surrounds us. Look around and appreciate the small details – the warmth of sunlight streaming through a window, the gentle breeze rustling leaves, or the sweet melody of birdsong. By training our minds to focus on these moments of wonder, we enhance our ability to tap into gratitude throughout the day.

As we dive deeper into the practice of daily gratitude, it's important to remain committed and consistent. Like any skill, gratitude deepens and becomes more impactful with regular practice. Embrace gratitude as a way of life, a daily nourishment for your soul, and watch as it transforms your mindset and attracts abundance into your life.

Remember, gratitude is not just about uttering a few words of thanks; it's a profound shift in perspective that influences our thoughts, actions, and emotions. It empowers us to embrace abundance and recognize the countless blessings we often take for granted. So, let us embark on this journey together, incorporating gratitude into our lives as a daily practice, and see the magic and transformation it brings.

In the second half of this chapter, we will delve deeper into the transformative power of gratitude as a daily practice. We will explore additional techniques and perspectives that can further enhance the abundance mindset that we are cultivating.

One powerful way to strengthen our gratitude practice is by incorporating mindfulness and meditation. By taking a few moments each day to sit in stillness, we can quiet the noise of our busy minds and tune into the present moment. During this time, we can focus our attention on gratitude, allowing ourselves to fully experience and appreciate the blessings in our lives. As we practice gratitude in this state of deep presence, we connect more intimately with the feelings of joy, contentment, and abundance.

Additionally, another beautiful way to infuse gratitude into our daily routine is by creating a gratitude jar. Find a jar or container and some small pieces of paper. Every day, write down something you are grateful for and place it in the jar. Over time, the jar will fill up with a collection of moments, experiences, and blessings that have brought you gratitude. When you're feeling down or in need of a boost, take a moment to sift through these notes and bask in the warmth and abundance they represent.

As we continue on this journey of gratitude, it is important to remember that challenges and difficulties are inevitable in life. However, by cultivating gratitude, we can navigate these moments with grace and resilience. Instead of seeing hardships as obstacles, we can view them as opportunities for growth and learning. Practice gratitude for the lessons learned during challenging times, and acknowledge the strength and courage that these experiences foster within us.

Furthermore, let us not forget the importance of self-gratitude. Often, we neglect to appreciate ourselves and the unique qualities and strengths we possess. Take a few moments each day to acknowledge your own achievements, talents, and efforts. Celebrate your progress and growth, no matter how small it may seem. By cultivating gratitude for ourselves, we strengthen our self-worth and confidence, allowing abundance to flow into our lives more effortlessly.

In addition to journaling, rituals, mindfulness, and self-appreciation, there is another powerful practice that can deepen our daily gratitude: the act of visualization. Spend a few minutes each day visualizing the life you desire, filled with abundance, joy, and fulfillment. See yourself surrounded by the people, experiences, and possessions that bring you happiness and gratitude. As you immerse yourself in this vision, feel the emotions of appreciation and abundance fill your heart. This practice of visualization not only enhances your gratitude but also acts as a powerful manifestation tool, bringing your desires into reality.

Lastly, as we conclude this chapter on gratitude as a daily practice, let us reflect on the incredible impact it can have on our overall well-being. By consistently acknowledging and appreciating the blessings in our lives, we shift our perspective from scarcity to abundance. We open ourselves up to receive more experiences, opportunities, and connections that align with our gratitude and amplify our sense of abundance.

Remember, gratitude is not a one-time practice or a temporary fix. It is a lifelong journey and a way of being. As we commit to incorporating this practice into our daily lives, we invite more joy, fulfillment, and prosperity into our existence. Embrace gratitude with an open heart and allow its transformative power to guide you on the path to a wealthy mindset filled with everlasting abundance.

So, my friend, as we come to the end of this chapter, take a moment to express gratitude for the knowledge and insights you have gained. Incorporate the practices that resonate with you into your daily routine, and embark on this journey of abundance and gratitude. May your life be filled with blessings, and may you continue to explore the art of instantaneous gratitude with an open heart and a wealth mindset.

Chapter 12: Gratitude Affirmations for Wealthy Mindset

When it comes to creating a wealthy mindset and attracting abundance effortlessly, one powerful tool that can make a significant difference in your life is gratitude affirmations. These powerful statements, when practiced regularly and sincerely, can shift your perspective, reprogram your subconscious mind, and enable you to manifest abundance with ease.

Gratitude affirmations allow you to focus your attention on the positive aspects of your life, no matter how big or small they may be. It's about acknowledging and appreciating the blessings and opportunities that surround you. By actively expressing gratitude, you invite more of these experiences into your life.

So, how can you create and utilize gratitude affirmations to reinforce a wealthy mindset? Let's explore some effective techniques that can transform your thoughts and beliefs:

1. Start with self-reflection: Take a moment to reflect on what you are genuinely grateful for in your life. It could be your health, relationships, career, or even simple pleasures like a beautiful sunset or the sound of laughter. Allow yourself to feel the gratitude deep within.

2. Be specific and genuine: When crafting your gratitude affirmations, be specific about what you appreciate. Instead of simply saying, "I am grateful for my job," specify why you are grateful. For example, "I am grateful for my fulfilling job that allows me to grow and contribute meaningfully."

3. Use present tense: Phrase your affirmations in the present tense to program your subconscious mind to believe and attract them into your reality. For instance, say, "I am grateful for the abundant opportunities that flow effortlessly into my life."

4. Embrace positive emotions: As you recite your gratitude affirmations, tap into the corresponding positive emotions. Feel the joy, love, and appreciation in your heart as you express your gratitude. This emotional connection amplifies the effectiveness of the affirmations.

5. Practice consistency: Make gratitude affirmations a part of your daily routine. Set aside a few minutes each day, whether in the morning or before bed, to affirm and express your gratitude. Consistency is key to reprogramming your mind and shaping a wealthy mindset.

6. Visualize abundance: As you recite your affirmations, visualize the abundance and wealth you desire. Imagine yourself living in that reality, feeling the happiness and fulfilment it brings. Use all your senses to make the visualization more vivid and powerful.

7. Share your gratitude: Extend your gratitude beyond yourself by appreciating and recognizing others. Express your thanks and appreciation to people who have made a positive impact on your life. This act of gratitude not only strengthens relationships but also attracts more abundance into your life.

By incorporating these techniques into your daily practice, you can harness the power of gratitude affirmations to cultivate a wealthy mindset. As you consistently focus on all the positive aspects of your life, you'll notice a shift in your perspective, enabling you to attract more abundance effortlessly.

Remember, gratitude is a mindset that can be cultivated with practice. It may take time, but as you continue to affirm your gratitude and embrace the emotions associated with it, you'll gradually align yourself with a wealthy mindset.

So, start today by creating your own gratitude affirmations. Write them down, say them out loud, and genuinely feel the gratitude within you. Allow these affirmations to become an integral part of your daily life, and watch as they unlock the doors to abundance and prosperity.

Now that you have learned the effective techniques for creating and utilizing gratitude affirmations to reinforce a wealthy mindset, it's time to dive deeper into the second half of this chapter. In this section, we will explore additional strategies and insights that can enhance the power of gratitude affirmations in attracting abundance effortlessly.

8. Amplify your affirmations with visualization: Visualization is a powerful tool that can align your thoughts, emotions, and desires with the reality you wish to manifest. As you recite your gratitude affirmations, take a moment to vividly visualize yourself living in a state of abundance. See yourself surrounded by wealth, success, and happiness. Allow yourself to feel the emotions associated with this visualization. By combining your gratitude affirmations with visualization, you create a potent cocktail for attracting abundance into your life.

9. Cultivate a daily gratitude practice: It's essential to make gratitude a daily practice in order to truly transform your mindset and attract abundance effortlessly. Set aside a few minutes each day to reflect on what you are grateful for and to recite your affirmations. This consistent practice reinforces the neural pathways in your brain, making gratitude a natural and effortless state of being. Remember, the more you practice gratitude, the more abundance you will attract into your life.

10. Write a gratitude journal: Another powerful way to cultivate gratitude is by keeping a gratitude journal. Take a few minutes each day to write down three to five things you are grateful for. By putting pen to paper, you strengthen the neural connections associated with gratitude and magnify its effects on your subconscious mind. Journaling also allows you to look back and reflect on the positive experiences and blessings that have enriched your life.

11. Surround yourself with gratitude reminders: Fill your environment with visual reminders of gratitude to reinforce your wealthy mindset. Place inspiring quotes, affirmations, or images that evoke feelings of gratitude around your home or workspace. These reminders serve as constant prompts to cultivate gratitude throughout your day and attract abundance effortlessly.

12. Practice gratitude in challenging times: Gratitude is not just about appreciating the good times; it's about finding the blessings even in challenging moments. When faced with difficulties or setbacks, train yourself to search for the lessons, growth opportunities, or unexpected silver linings within them. By embracing a mindset of gratitude, even during tough times, you can shift your perspective and attract positive outcomes.

13. Embrace generosity and giving: Gratitude and abundance are intimately linked with generosity. Cultivate a giving mindset by offering your time, resources, or kind gestures to others. When you give freely and without expectation, you reinforce the belief that you have an abundance to share. By practicing generosity, you create a flow of abundance that comes back to you multiplied.

14. Release attachments and trust the process: While gratitude affirmations are a powerful tool for manifesting abundance, it's important to release attachments to specific outcomes. Trust that the universe has a plan for you and that the abundance you desire will come in the perfect timing and form. Detach from expectations and surrender to the flow of divine abundance, knowing that what is meant for you will always find its way.

15. Celebrate and acknowledge your progress: As you continue to practice gratitude affirmations and cultivate a wealthy mindset, celebrate and acknowledge the progress you have made. Recognize the shifts in your perspective, the opportunities that have come your way, and the abundance that has already manifested in your life. By

celebrating small wins and acknowledging your growth, you amplify the positive energy of gratitude and attract even more abundance.

Remember, mastering the art of instantaneous gratitude for a wealthy mindset is an ongoing journey. It requires consistent practice, patience, and a willingness to transform your thoughts and beliefs. By incorporating these strategies into your daily life, you will continue to strengthen your gratitude muscle and attract abundance effortlessly.

As we conclude this chapter, take a moment to reflect on how you can integrate gratitude affirmations into your daily routine. What techniques resonate with you the most? How can you make gratitude a natural and effortless part of your mindset? Trust in the power of gratitude and embark on this journey with an open heart. The abundance you seek is already within you; it's simply a matter of unlocking its full potential through the practice of gratitude.

Chapter 13: Cultivating an Attitude of Generosity

Generosity is a powerful force that has the ability to transform our lives in ways we might not even imagine. When we think of abundance and wealth, the concept of generosity might not be the first thing that comes to mind. However, practicing generosity can be the key to unlocking a wealthy mindset and attracting more opportunities and wealth into our lives.

So, what exactly does it mean to cultivate an attitude of generosity? It goes beyond just giving material possessions or money. It is about embracing a mindset that is open to sharing, giving, and serving others. Cultivating this attitude of generosity not only benefits those around us but also has a profound impact on our own well-being and abundance.

One of the simplest ways to start cultivating an attitude of generosity is by practicing gratitude. When we are grateful for what we have, we become more aware of the abundance already present in our lives. This shift in perspective allows us to see the value in sharing and giving to others. It helps us recognize that generosity is not about scarcity or loss, but about creating a ripple effect of positive energy and abundance.

When we give from a place of genuine generosity, we tap into the universal law of reciprocity. This law states that the energy we put out into the world comes back to us in various forms. When we give generously, whether it is our time, resources, or skills, we create a flow of abundance that attracts more opportunities, wealth, and blessings into our lives.

Practicing generosity also helps us cultivate a mindset of abundance rather than scarcity. Scarcity thinking is rooted in the belief that there is not enough to go around, leading to feelings of fear, lack, and competition. On the other hand, generosity thinking embraces the belief that there is an abundance of resources, opportunities, and wealth available for everyone.

As we shift our mindset from scarcity to abundance, we begin to see the world through a different lens. We focus on possibilities rather than limitations, and we attract more opportunities and wealth into our lives. When we are generous, we operate from a place of trust and faith, knowing that by giving, we are aligning ourselves with the flow of abundance in the universe.

Moreover, generosity opens doors for us. When we are known for our generosity, people are more likely to support us and offer us opportunities that we may not have otherwise received. As we give freely and without expectation, we create a network of positive energy and goodwill that can manifest in surprising and unexpected ways.

In addition to attracting wealth and opportunities, cultivating an attitude of generosity also brings immense joy and fulfillment into our lives. The act of giving creates a deep sense of purpose and connection with others. It allows us to make a positive difference in the lives of those around us, and in turn, uplifts our own spirits.

As we embark on this journey of cultivating an attitude of generosity, let us remember that it is not about how much we give, but rather the intention and sincerity behind our actions. Generosity can manifest in various forms, whether it is volunteering our time, sharing our knowledge, or simply offering a listening ear to someone in need. Every act of generosity, no matter how small, has the power to create a ripple effect of abundance and transformation.

In the second half of this chapter, we will explore practical strategies and exercises to help you cultivate a daily practice of generosity and integrate it into every aspect of your life. Get ready to discover powerful techniques that will amplify your abundance mindset and attract even more wealth and opportunities. Get ready to unlock the true potential of generosity and experience the transformative power it holds. But until then, let us reflect on the impact of a generous mindset, and the possibilities that lie ahead when we embrace the art of giving. As we continue our exploration of cultivating an attitude of generosity, let's dive deeper into the practical strategies and exercises that can help us integrate this mindset into every aspect of our lives.

One powerful way to cultivate a daily practice of generosity is by becoming more mindful of our thoughts, words, and actions. Pay attention to moments throughout the day when you can extend kindness, offer help, or simply be present for someone in need. It could be as simple as holding the door open for someone, offering a genuine compliment, or actively listening to a friend who needs a supportive ear. By consciously choosing to show generosity in these small moments, we begin to shift our mindset from scarcity to abundance.

Another effective strategy is to create a giving plan. Take some time to reflect on your passions, talents, and resources. How can you leverage these to make a positive impact in your community? Whether it's volunteering at a local charity, mentoring someone in need, or contributing to a cause you deeply care about, creating a plan will help you focus your efforts and maximize your impact. Remember, generosity is not just about money or material possessions; it's about offering your time, skills, and expertise to uplift others.

Practicing generosity in our relationships is also crucial. Relationships are built on a foundation of trust, respect, and mutual support. Actively showing generosity towards others helps strengthen these bonds and creates a network of positive energy. It could be as simple as offering a helping hand to a colleague, being supportive of a friend's dreams and aspirations, or expressing gratitude for the people in your life. By nurturing these connections through acts of generosity, we not only uplift others but also create a positive environment that fosters growth and abundance.

Furthermore, let us not forget the importance of self-care in cultivating an attitude of generosity. Taking care of our own physical, mental, and emotional well-being allows us to show up fully for others. Remember the saying, "You cannot pour from an empty cup." By prioritizing self-care, we are able to replenish ourselves and have more to give to others. Practice self-compassion, engage in activities that bring you joy, and set healthy boundaries to ensure a balanced and sustainable approach to generosity.

Lastly, practicing gratitude continues to be an essential component of cultivating an attitude of generosity. Regularly take time to reflect on the abundance in your life and express gratitude for the blessings you have received. Gratitude amplifies the positive energy and abundance within us, making it easier to share and give to others. Consider starting a gratitude journal or participating in a daily gratitude practice to cultivate a deeper sense of appreciation and generosity.

As we conclude this chapter on cultivating an attitude of generosity, let us embrace the transformational power that it holds. Remember, generosity is not about the quantity of what we give, but rather the intention and sincerity behind our actions. Every act of generosity, no matter how small, has the potential to create a ripple effect of abundance and positive transformation.

By integrating the practices and strategies discussed in this chapter into our daily lives, we will continue to amplify our abundance mindset and attract even more wealth and opportunities. The journey of generosity is a lifelong process, and as we continue on this path, let us remain open and receptive to the infinite possibilities that lie ahead.

With each act of generosity, we not only make a difference in the lives of others but also cultivate fulfillment, joy, and purpose within ourselves. So, let us continue to embrace the art of giving and experience the profound impact it has on our lives and the world around us.

As we move forward on our journey towards a wealthy mindset, let generosity be our guiding principle, and let us always strive to create a world filled with abundance, love, and kindness.

Chapter 14: Gratitude in the Face of Challenges

Life is full of challenges. We all encounter hardships and obstacles along our journey, but it is how we respond to these challenges that truly defines us. In times of adversity, it can be easy to get consumed by negativity and despair. However, by cultivating a mindset of gratitude, we can navigate through difficult situations with resilience and bounce back stronger towards abundance.

Gratitude is a powerful tool that allows us to shift our focus from scarcity to abundance. When we express gratitude, we acknowledge the blessings we have in our lives, even amidst challenges. It helps us cultivate a positive outlook, enabling us to see beyond the obstacles and embrace the opportunities that lie ahead.

During tough times, it may feel counterintuitive to be grateful. Our instinct may be to dwell on the things that go wrong or to fixate on what we lack. But in doing so, we overlook the valuable lessons and growth opportunities that challenges present. It is through these difficult experiences that we develop resilience, strength, and wisdom. By practicing gratitude, we can uncover the hidden blessings within our challenges.

One way gratitude can help us navigate through tough times is by fostering a mindset of abundance. When we focus on what we are grateful for, we shift our attention away from scarcity and limitations. Instead, we become aware of the abundance that surrounds us, allowing us to tap into the infinite possibilities that await us.

In the face of challenges, gratitude acts as a guiding light, illuminating the path towards solutions and new beginnings. It empowers us to search for silver linings, no matter how small they may seem. Whether it is finding strength in the support of loved ones or discovering new opportunities for growth, gratitude helps us find hope and keep moving forward.

Moreover, gratitude serves as a powerful tool for reframing our perspective. When we practice gratitude, we challenge the negative narratives that can often dominate our thoughts during difficult times. By consciously focusing on what we are grateful for, we override the tendency to ruminate on our problems, allowing space for positive energy and solutions to emerge.

Furthermore, gratitude has a profound effect on our overall well-being. Research has shown that practicing gratitude can improve mental health, increase happiness, and reduce stress. In times of challenges, our mental and emotional well-being can be greatly impacted. However, by incorporating gratitude into our daily lives, we foster a sense of resilience and emotional balance, enabling us to face adversity with a healthier mindset.

As we navigate through challenges, it is important to remember that gratitude is not about denying or dismissing the hardships we face. It is about acknowledging the difficult emotions that arise and choosing to shift our focus towards gratitude and abundance. It is a conscious decision to find strength and meaning in the face of adversity.

In the second half of this chapter, we will delve deeper into specific strategies and practices that can help us cultivate gratitude in the midst of challenges. Together, we will explore practical exercises and tools that can empower us to embrace a mindset of gratitude and bounce back stronger towards abundance.

But for now, let us reflect on the power of gratitude in the face of challenges. How has gratitude helped you navigate through difficult times in the past? Have you discovered unexpected blessings amidst adversity? Take a moment to appreciate the resilience and strength that has brought you this far.

Remember, challenges are not setbacks but opportunities for growth. As we continue our journey towards abundance, let us embrace the power of gratitude and discover the transformative potential it holds.

And with that, we leave you, suspended in anticipation for the second half of this chapter, where we will unveil practical strategies to harness the power of gratitude in times of adversity. Stay tuned for the continuation of our exploration, and get ready to unlock the full potential of a grateful mindset. In the second half of this chapter, we will delve deeper into specific strategies and practices that can help us cultivate gratitude in the midst of challenges. These practical exercises and tools will empower us to embrace a mindset of gratitude and bounce back stronger towards abundance.

One powerful strategy for cultivating gratitude in challenging times is to keep a gratitude journal. This involves setting aside a few minutes each day to write down three things you are grateful for. These could be big or small blessings, such as a supportive friend, a beautiful sunset, or a delicious meal. By actively seeking out moments of gratitude, we train our minds to focus on the positive aspects of our lives, even in the face of difficulties.

Another effective practice is to create a gratitude jar. Find a jar and some strips of colored paper. Whenever you experience a moment of gratitude or receive kindness from someone, write it down on a strip of paper and place it in the jar. Over time, the jar will fill up with reminders of the blessings in your life. On those tough days, you can pull out a few strips and read them as a reminder of the goodness that surrounds you.

In addition to these practices, it is important to consciously choose our perspective. When faced with challenges, we can either focus on what is lacking or embrace gratitude for what we have. By shifting our attention towards abundance, we open ourselves up to new possibilities and solutions. Instead of dwelling on what went wrong, we can learn from our experiences and find gratitude for the lessons they teach us.

Another powerful strategy is to reach out and show gratitude to others. During tough times, it is easy to become self-centered and withdraw from social interactions. However, by expressing gratitude to those around us, we not only strengthen our relationships but also cultivate a positive mindset. A simple thank you note or a heartfelt conversation can go a long way in fostering a sense of connection and gratitude.

Practicing self-compassion is also crucial in cultivating gratitude during challenging times. It is important to acknowledge and validate our own emotions, even if they are difficult. By being kind to ourselves and treating ourselves with compassion, we create a nurturing environment for gratitude to flourish. This can involve self-care practices such as meditation, exercise, or engaging in hobbies that bring us joy.

Lastly, it is important to remember that gratitude is a practice, and it takes time to develop. Like any skill, it requires consistent effort and repetition. As you embark on this journey of cultivating gratitude, be patient with yourself and celebrate even the small victories. Each step towards a grateful mindset brings you closer to embracing abundance in the face of challenges.

In conclusion, cultivating gratitude in the face of challenges is a transformative journey that requires conscious effort and practice. By incorporating strategies such as keeping a gratitude journal, creating a gratitude jar, choosing our perspective, expressing gratitude to others, practicing self-compassion, and celebrating the small victories, we can harness the power of gratitude to navigate through tough times and bounce back stronger towards abundance.

Now, take a moment to reflect on the strategies that resonate with you. How can you incorporate them into your daily life? What steps will you take to deepen your practice of gratitude? Remember, you have the power to transform your mindset and embrace a grateful perspective, even in the midst of challenges. Stay committed to this journey, and you will unlock the full potential of a grateful mindset, paving the way for abundance and prosperity. Keep practicing, stay resilient, and let gratitude guide you towards a wealthy mindset.

Chapter 15: The Connection Between Health and Wealth

Uncover the correlation between physical and mental well-being and your ability to cultivate an abundant mindset.

When it comes to wealth, many people solely focus on financial aspects. They strive to acquire more money, believing it will lead to happiness and fulfillment. While wealth can certainly provide opportunities and security, it is essential to recognize the connection between health and wealth. The state of our physical and mental well-being plays a significant role in our ability to create and maintain abundance in our lives.

A healthy body and mind form the foundation upon which we can build a wealthy mindset. Without good health, it becomes challenging to pursue our goals and aspirations. We feel depleted, lacking the necessary energy and motivation to go after what we desire. In contrast, when we prioritize our well-being, we pave the way for abundance in all areas of life.

Physical health is often underestimated when discussing wealth, but its impact cannot be ignored. Ignoring our bodies' needs can lead to health issues that hinder our ability to thrive in various aspects of life. Imagine trying to focus on building wealth when your body is constantly fatigued or in pain. It's challenging, if not impossible, to be productive and make informed decisions.

Taking care of our physical health involves adopting healthy eating habits, engaging in regular exercise, and getting enough rest. Eating a well-balanced diet not only provides our bodies with essential nutrients but also impacts our cognitive functions. When we fuel ourselves with nourishing foods, we experience increased mental clarity, enabling us to make better financial decisions.

Exercise, on the other hand, boosts our energy levels, strengthens our immune system, and improves our overall well-being. Engaging in physical activity releases endorphins, commonly known as the "feel-good" hormone, which helps reduce stress and anxiety. By incorporating exercise into our daily routine, we increase our mental resilience and fortify ourselves against the challenges that may arise on our journey to wealth.

Furthermore, sleep plays a crucial role in our physical and mental health. Getting sufficient rest allows our bodies to repair and rejuvenate, ensuring we wake up refreshed and ready to tackle the day's challenges. A lack of sleep can lead to decreased cognitive function, impaired decision-making skills, and increased stress levels. To operate at our best and cultivate an abundant mindset, prioritizing quality sleep is essential.

While physical health sets the stage for wealth creation, mental well-being acts as the driving force behind it. Our thoughts, beliefs, and attitudes have a significant impact on our ability to attract and manifest abundance. Cultivating a positive mindset opens us up to new possibilities and helps us overcome obstacles along the way.

Practicing gratitude is a powerful tool in shifting our mindset from scarcity to abundance. When we acknowledge and appreciate the blessings in our lives, we attract more positive experiences and opportunities for wealth. Gratitude breeds contentment and enables us to focus on what we have rather than what we lack.

Moreover, managing stress and cultivating resilience are essential in navigating the ups and downs of wealth creation. Developing effective stress management techniques, such as meditation, deep breathing exercises, and mindfulness, allows us to maintain clarity and focus.

These practices enhance our decision-making abilities, ultimately leading to more fruitful outcomes.

In conclusion, the connection between health and wealth goes beyond mere financial success. To cultivate an abundant mindset, we must prioritize our physical and mental well-being. Taking care of our bodies through healthy eating, exercise, and sleep provides us with the energy and vitality needed to pursue wealth. Simultaneously, maintaining a positive mindset, practicing gratitude, and managing stress are crucial in attracting and manifesting abundance. By recognizing the correlation between health and wealth, we can set ourselves on a path to true prosperity.

To truly master the art of instantaneous gratitude for a wealthy mindset, we need to understand the importance of self-care. One aspect of self-care that often gets overlooked is our emotional well-being. Our emotions play a significant role in shaping our mindset, influencing our decisions, and ultimately impacting our ability to create wealth.

Developing emotional intelligence is crucial in cultivating a wealthy mindset. It involves recognizing and understanding our emotions, as well as effectively managing them. When we are aware of our emotions, we can respond to challenging situations with clarity and composure, rather than reacting impulsively.

One powerful tool for enhancing emotional intelligence is self-reflection. Taking the time to explore our thoughts and feelings allows us to gain insight into ourselves and uncover any limiting beliefs that may be holding us back from abundance. By replacing negative self-talk with empowering affirmations, we can shift our mindset from scarcity to abundance.

In addition to emotional intelligence, building and maintaining strong relationships is key to our overall well-being and wealth creation. Our connections with others can provide support, guidance, and valuable opportunities. Nurturing these relationships requires effective communication, active listening, and genuine empathy.

Moreover, surrounding ourselves with like-minded individuals who share our goals and aspirations can inspire us and keep us accountable. Joining mastermind groups or seeking out mentors can provide valuable insights and motivation on our journey to wealth.

Another essential aspect of cultivating an abundant mindset is continuous learning. In the rapidly changing world we live in, it is crucial to stay updated and adapt to new opportunities. Investing in our personal and professional development opens doors to growth and expands our capacity to generate wealth.

Reading books, attending seminars, or engaging in online courses that align with our goals can provide us with valuable knowledge and skills. The more we invest in ourselves, the more we can bring to the table in terms of value, ideas, and opportunities.

Furthermore, to unleash our creative potential and tap into innovative ideas, we must embrace the power of imagination. Visualization and meditation techniques can help us unlock our subconscious mind, allowing us to see possibilities beyond our current reality. As we visualize our desired outcomes and connect with the emotions associated with achieving them, we align ourselves with the abundance we seek.

Finally, giving back to others is an integral part of a wealthy mindset. Helping those in need, contributing to meaningful causes, and practicing acts of kindness not only improve the lives of others but also bring fulfillment and gratitude into our own lives. By sharing our wealth—whether it be time, knowledge, or resources—we attract more wealth and abundance into our own lives.

In conclusion, the second half of Chapter 15 emphasizes the importance of emotional intelligence, building strong relationships, continuous learning, embracing imagination, and giving back as key components of cultivating a wealthy mindset. By integrating these practices into our lives, we pave the way for abundance in all its forms.

Remember, the path to wealth is not solely about financial success but encompasses our physical and mental well-being, emotional intelligence, relationships, continuous learning, imagination, and giving back. We must strive for true prosperity by prioritizing these aspects of our lives and nurturing a wealthy mindset.

In the subsequent chapters, we will explore various other aspects related to transforming scarcity into abundance. From practical strategies to mindset shifts, we'll continue to delve deeper into the art of instantaneous gratitude for a wealthy mindset. So, stay tuned for more insights and practical advice to support your journey towards unlimited abundance.

Chapter 16: Breaking Free from Comparison

Comparison is a powerful force that has the ability to hold us back from living a fulfilled and abundant life. It's easy to get caught up in the trap of comparing ourselves to others, whether it be their achievements, possessions, or even their physical appearance. But the truth is, comparison only serves to rob us of our own joy and hinder our progress on the path to abundance.

In a world that is constantly bombarding us with images of success and perfection, it's no wonder that we find ourselves falling into the comparison trap. We scroll through social media feeds filled with carefully curated lives, feeling inadequate and envious of what others have accomplished. But what we fail to realize is that these comparisons are not only unfair to ourselves, but also to the individuals we are comparing ourselves to.

When we compare ourselves to others, we are comparing our internal struggles and challenges to someone else's highlight reel. We only see the edited version of their lives, the successes, and the accomplishments that they choose to share. We forget that behind those achievements, there may be countless failures, sacrifices, and hard work. We forget that everyone has their own unique journey and that success is not a one-size-fits-all concept.

To break free from the comparison trap, we must shift our focus from others to ourselves. Instead of constantly measuring our worth against someone else's, we need to embrace our own journey and celebrate our own progress. This begins with cultivating a mindset of gratitude and self-compassion.

Gratitude is the foundation of abundance. When we learn to appreciate what we already have, we shift our focus from scarcity to abundance. Take a moment to reflect on all the blessings in your life – the relationships, experiences, and opportunities that have shaped who you are today. By acknowledging and expressing gratitude for these blessings, we create a sense of abundance within ourselves.

Self-compassion is another powerful tool in overcoming comparison. Instead of berating ourselves for not measuring up to someone else's standards, we need to practice self-kindness and understanding. We are all human, and we all have flaws and imperfections. Instead of dwelling on what we lack, let's focus on our strengths and the areas where we excel. Understanding that everyone has their own unique journey will help us break free from the cycle of comparison and embrace our own path to abundance.

One effective strategy to overcome comparison is to shift our perspective and focus on collaboration rather than competition. Instead of viewing others as rivals, let's see them as potential allies and sources of inspiration. By building a supportive network of like-minded individuals, we can learn from each other, share experiences, and celebrate each other's successes. Collaboration not only fosters a sense of connectedness but also opens up new opportunities and expands our own horizons.

As we continue our journey from scarcity to abundance, it's important to remember that comparison is a choice. We have the power to choose how we perceive ourselves and others. We can choose to be grateful for what we have, practice self-compassion, and embrace collaboration. By doing so, we allow ourselves to focus on our own abundance journey and truly experience a wealthy mindset.

In the second half of this chapter, we will delve deeper into practical strategies to overcome comparison and envy. We will explore ways to shift our mindset, set meaningful goals, and cultivate a sense of contentment. Stay tuned for the next part, where we will guide you through the steps towards breaking free from comparison and embracing the abundance that is waiting for you. In the second half of this chapter, we will delve deeper into practical strategies to overcome comparison and envy. We will explore ways to shift our mindset, set meaningful goals, and cultivate a sense of contentment. So, without further ado, let's continue our journey of breaking free from comparison and embracing the abundance that is waiting for you.

One powerful strategy to overcome comparison is to practice self-awareness. By becoming aware of our thoughts and emotions when we compare ourselves to others, we can begin to challenge those beliefs and replace them with more empowering ones. When you find yourself comparing, take a moment to pause and ask yourself, "Is this comparison helpful or serving me in any way?" Often, you'll realize that comparing only creates feelings of inadequacy and dissatisfaction. By acknowledging this, you can consciously choose to shift your focus back to your own journey and progress.

Another effective method to conquer comparison is to celebrate the success and accomplishments of others genuinely. Instead of feeling envious or resentful, choose to congratulate and cheer for them wholeheartedly. By doing so, you shift from a scarcity mindset to an abundance mindset. Recognize that someone else's success does not diminish your own. In fact, by celebrating their achievements, you create an atmosphere of positivity and support, which can inspire and motivate you on your own path to abundance.

Furthermore, it's crucial to set meaningful goals for yourself. Rather than comparing your progress to someone else's, focus on what you want to achieve and create a plan to get there. Make your goals specific, measurable, attainable, relevant, and time-bound (SMART goals). When you have a clear vision of where you're headed, it becomes easier to stay focused on your own journey and not get caught up in comparing yourself to others. Remember that success is not a race, but a personal journey filled with growth and learning.

Cultivating a sense of contentment is another key element in breaking free from comparison. Practice gratitude regularly by keeping a gratitude journal or simply listing three things you're grateful for each day. This simple act of gratitude shifts your focus from what you lack to what you have, creating a mindset of abundance. Additionally, make an effort to be present in the present moment and appreciate the journey you're on. Embrace the ups and downs, the challenges and victories, for they are all part of your unique story. By finding contentment in where you are right now, you can fully embrace your own abundant life without comparing it to others.

Lastly, surround yourself with a supportive network of like-minded individuals who uplift and inspire you. Seek out mentors, join groups or communities, and engage in conversations that encourage growth and positivity. By surrounding yourself with people who are on a similar journey, you can share experiences, learn from one another, and celebrate each other's successes. Collaboration fosters a sense of connectedness and expands your own horizons, helping you realize that we are all in this together.

As you embark on the path of breaking free from comparison, remember that it is a continuous process. Some days will be easier than others, but with practice and persistence, you can develop a mindset that is focused on your own abundance and growth. Embrace your uniqueness, appreciate what you have, and set meaningful goals that align with your values and purpose. Comparison will no longer have power over you as you step into your own journey of abundance and gratitude.

In conclusion, comparison is a trap that robs us of joy and hinder our progress towards abundance. By shifting our focus from others to ourselves, practicing self-compassion, celebrating the success of others, setting meaningful goals, cultivating contentment, and building a supportive network, we can break free from comparison and embrace our own path to abundance. So, let go of comparison, embrace your uniqueness, and allow gratitude and collaboration to guide you towards a wealthy mindset. Keep moving forward on your journey, for the true wealth lies in the journey itself.

Chapter 17: Gratitude Practices for Financial Abundance

In our journey to cultivating a wealthy mindset, we have explored various practices that help us shift from scarcity to abundance. We have learned how gratitude can transform our lives, bringing joy, contentment, and an attitude of appreciation into every facet of our existence. Now, let's take a closer look at gratitude practices specifically tailored to attract financial abundance and transform our relationship with money.

1. Daily Money Gratitude Journal:

Imagine starting your day with a cup of coffee and a few minutes dedicated to reflecting on the abundance of money in your life. Take out your journal and write down five things you are grateful for regarding your finances. It could be as simple as having a roof over your head, a steady income, or the ability to afford your favorite indulgence. By consistently recognizing the financial blessings around you, you set the tone for attracting even more abundance into your life.

2. Visualizing Financial Goals:

Visualization is a powerful tool that can help manifest your desires. Take a moment to close your eyes and imagine your ideal financial situation. See yourself surrounded by wealth and financial security. Engage all your senses, envisioning the experiences you wish to have. By regularly visualizing your financial goals, you align your thoughts and actions with the abundant reality you seek to create.

3. Gratitude Affirmations:

Affirmations are positive statements that reinforce your beliefs and intentions. Craft a few affirmations that emphasize abundance and gratitude for your financial journey. Repeat them to yourself daily, allowing the words to sink deep into your subconscious mind. For example, say, "I am grateful for the wealth that flows into my life effortlessly" or "I appreciate the abundance of money that supports all my desires and dreams."

4. Giving Back:

It may seem counterintuitive, but giving back can create a powerful flow of financial abundance in your life. Find a cause or organization that resonates with you and make a regular practice of donating your time, money, or resources. As you give, you express gratitude for the wealth you already possess, which opens up space for even more to come your way.

5. Gratitude Walk:

Take a walk-in nature and let gratitude infuse your senses. As you stroll, express gratitude for the natural abundance surrounding you. Observe the trees providing oxygen, the sunlight warming your skin, and the vibrant colors of flowers offering beauty to the world. By immersing yourself in gratitude while connecting with nature, you tap into the limitless abundance of the universe.

6. Abundance Visualization Meditation:

Set aside some quiet time for a gratitude visualization meditation. Find a comfortable position, close your eyes, and focus on your breath. As you inhale and exhale, imagine a golden light enveloping your body and filling you with gratitude for your financial blessings. Visualize this light expanding, radiating abundance from within you, attracting more prosperity into your life.

7. Appreciating Micro-Abundance:

Often, we overlook the small moments of financial abundance that occur daily. Take a moment to appreciate the free cup of coffee a friend treats you to, finding a coin on the ground, or discovering a great discount on something you need. Cultivate a habit of noticing and acknowledging these micro-abundances, for they add up and align you with the energy of prosperity.

Now, you might be wondering, how do these gratitude practices specifically attract financial abundance? How can they transform our relationship with money? Stay tuned for the second half of this chapter, where we will explore the deeper mechanisms behind these practices and uncover the secrets to harnessing wealth through gratitude. But for now, embrace the gratitude practices shared in this first half and experience their transformative power in your financial journey.

Remember, your mindset is the key to unlocking a wealthy life. By embracing gratitude and utilizing these practices tailored for attracting financial abundance, you are paving the way to financial freedom and a wealthier future. So, keep an open mind, stay committed to your journey, and get ready to uncover the true power of gratitude in the realm of money.

- -So far, we have delved into various gratitude practices specifically tailored to attract financial abundance and transform our relationship with money. These practices have the power to shift our mindset, create positive energy, and attract wealth into our lives. In the first half of this chapter, we explored daily money gratitude journaling, visualizing financial goals, gratitude affirmations, giving back, gratitude walks, abundance visualization meditation, and appreciating micro-abundance.

Now, let's dive deeper into the mechanisms behind these practices and uncover the secrets of harnessing wealth through gratitude.

First and foremost, gratitude practices shift our focus from scarcity to abundance. When we express gratitude for the financial blessings we already have, we send a powerful signal to the universe that we are open to receiving more. It is like creating a magnetic force that attracts abundance into our lives. By consistently recognizing the wealth and resources around us, we shift our perspective and begin to view money as a tool for creating the life we desire.

The daily money gratitude journal, for example, helps us cultivate a habit of gratitude specifically towards our finances. By writing down five things we are grateful for regarding our finances every morning, we start our day with a positive mindset, appreciating the monetary blessings we have. This practice sets the tone for attracting even more financial abundance into our lives because we attract what we focus on.

Visualizing our financial goals is another powerful practice. When we engage all our senses and immerse ourselves in the experience of achieving our financial desires, we create a vivid image in our minds. This image acts as a blueprint for our subconscious mind and guides our thoughts, actions, and decisions towards manifesting our goals. By consistently visualizing our financial abundance, we align ourselves with the energy of abundance and attract opportunities that lead us closer to our desired outcomes.

Gratitude affirmations further reinforce the beliefs and intentions we have towards financial abundance. By crafting positive statements and repeating them daily, we reprogram our subconscious mind to align with our desires. These affirmations, such as "I am grateful for the wealth that flows into my life effortlessly," or "I appreciate the abundance of money that supports all my desires and dreams," help us shift our mindset from lack to abundance. They remind us to focus on the positive aspects of our financial journey, creating a mindset of gratitude and attracting more wealth into our lives.

Giving back is another practice that may seem counterintuitive to attracting financial abundance. However, when we give, whether it's our time, money, or resources, we create a flow of positive energy and gratitude. By expressing gratitude for the wealth, we already possess, we open up space for more to come our way. Giving back allows us to share our abundance with others, and as we do so, we generate a sense of fulfillment and purpose. This positive energy attracts more wealth into our lives, as the universe rewards our generosity.

Gratitude walks offer a unique opportunity to transform our relationship with money by connecting with nature. As we immerse ourselves in the beauty and abundance of the natural world, we tap into the limitless abundance of the universe. By expressing gratitude for the oxygen-producing trees, the soothing sunlight, and the vibrant colors of flowers, we cultivate a deep appreciation for the natural abundance that surrounds us. This sense of connection and gratitude expands our awareness of the wealth available to us in all its forms.

Abundance visualization meditation allows us to take a sacred pause and connect with the gratitude within us. As we focus on our breath and visualize a golden light filling us with gratitude for our financial blessings, we align our energy with the energy of abundance. This meditation practice helps us release any limiting beliefs or fears about money and opens us up to receive the wealth that is available to us.

Lastly, appreciating micro-abundance reminds us to notice and acknowledge the small moments of financial abundance that occur daily. These micro-abundances may seem insignificant, but they add up and align us with the energy of prosperity. By expressing gratitude for a friend treating us to a free cup of coffee, finding a coin on the ground, or discovering a great discount, we train our minds to focus on the positive aspects of our financial journey. This cultivates a mindset of gratitude and attracts more abundance into our lives.

In conclusion, these gratitude practices are powerful tools for attracting financial abundance and transforming our relationship with money. They shift our focus from scarcity to abundance, align our thoughts and actions with our desires, and create a positive energy that attracts wealth into our lives. So, continue to embrace these practices, and witness the transformative power of gratitude unfold in your financial journey. Remember, a wealthy mindset starts with gratitude, and through these practices, you are opening the doors to a wealthier future. Trust in the process, stay committed, and watch as the universe responds to your gratitude with abundant blessings.

Chapter 18: Embracing Abundance in Every Area of Life

Have you ever wondered what it truly means to live an abundant life? Is it solely defined by the size of our bank accounts, the number of possessions we accumulate, or the material wealth we have? Or could there be something more to it, a deeper and more profound way of experiencing abundance? In this chapter, we will delve into the concept of abundance and explore how it extends beyond just financial wealth, enriching every aspect of our lives.

When we think about abundance, our minds often tend to gravitate towards money and material possessions. It's no surprise considering how our society places such strong emphasis on these aspects. However, true abundance is not limited to financial prosperity. It encompasses our relationships, health, personal growth, and overall well-being. It is about cultivating a mindset and lifestyle that embraces abundance in all areas of life.

So, how can we expand our mindset of abundance beyond just financial wealth? One way is by cultivating a practice of gratitude. Gratitude is the key that unlocks the doors to abundance in every area of our lives. When we shift our focus from what we lack to what we have, we invite more blessings and abundance into our experience. By acknowledging and appreciating the abundance that already exists, we open ourselves to receiving even more.

Practicing gratitude is not about denying the challenges or difficulties we may face. It is about consciously choosing to shift our perspective and find something to be grateful for in every situation. It is about training our minds to see the positive aspects of our lives and to recognize the countless blessings we often take for granted. When we embrace a mindset of gratitude, we align ourselves with the flow of abundance and start attracting more of it into our lives.

Another powerful way to embrace abundance in every area of life is by adopting an abundance mindset. This mindset is rooted in the belief that there is always more than enough to go around. It is the understanding that the universe is abundant, and we are deserving of all the good things it has to offer. By letting go of scarcity and lack mentality, we create space for abundance to flow into our lives.

An abundance mindset goes hand in hand with a mindset of possibilities and opportunities. It is about shifting our focus from limitations to endless potential. When we believe that opportunities are abundant, we become more open to exploring new paths, taking risks, and stepping outside our comfort zones. We start to see setbacks as stepping stones towards growth and learn to embrace the lessons they bring. With an abundance mindset, we approach life with a sense of curiosity, excitement, and confidence, knowing that we are capable of creating our own abundance.

As we expand our mindset of abundance, we begin to experience a more fulfilled and enriched life as a whole. Our relationships become deeper and more meaningful as we appreciate the abundance of love and connections around us. Our health and well-being improve as we recognize the abundance of vitality and energy within us. Our personal growth soars as we tap into the abundance of knowledge and wisdom available to us. We become the masters of this art of instantaneous gratitude, creating a wealthy mindset that extends far beyond monetary wealth.

In conclusion... Oh wait, there is no conclusion in this first half of the chapter! We will leave you hanging right here, eagerly anticipating the second half. So, stay tuned as we dive even deeper into embracing abundance in every area of life. There's so much more to discover, and we can't wait to continue this exciting journey with you! In the previous section, we discussed the importance of gratitude and cultivating an abundance mindset in order to embrace abundance in every area of life. Now, let's dive even deeper into this journey of abundance and explore some practical strategies to help us manifest and attract more abundance into our lives.

One powerful tool for embracing abundance is visualization. The power of our imagination is limitless, and by visualizing our desired outcomes, we can begin to manifest them. Take a moment to close your eyes and imagine yourself in a state of abundance. What does that look like to you? How do you feel in this state of abundance? Allow yourself to fully immerse in these feelings and sensations. Let go of any doubts or limitations that may arise and believe in the possibility of abundance in your life.

Visualization goes hand in hand with setting clear and specific goals. When we have a clear vision of what we want to manifest, we can take inspired action towards its achievement. Write down your goals and create a plan of action to bring them to fruition. Break them down into smaller, actionable steps that you can take each day. Taking consistent action towards your goals will not only bring you closer to them but also reinforce your belief in the abundance available to you.

Alongside visualization and goal setting, it is essential to cultivate a mindset of trust and surrender. Trust that the universe is always conspiring in your favor and that everything is unfolding for your highest good. Trust that the abundance you desire is already on its way to you. Surrender the need for control and allow the universe to guide you towards your desires. By letting go of the need to micromanage every aspect of your life, you create space for miracles and unexpected opportunities to show up.

Another powerful practice to embrace abundance in every area of life is to surround yourself with positive and supportive influences. The people we spend time with and the information we consume greatly impact our mindset and beliefs. Surround yourself with individuals who uplift and inspire you, who believe in your dreams, and who encourage your growth. Seek out mentors, coaches, or like-minded individuals who have achieved the abundance you desire, and learn from their experiences.

In addition to the outer influences, nurturing self-care practices is crucial for embracing abundance. Take care of your physical, mental, and emotional well-being. Prioritize activities that bring you joy and nourish your soul. This can be anything from meditation, exercise, journaling, spending time in nature, or indulging in creative pursuits. Remember that self-care is not selfish; it is an act of self-love and self-respect, which in turn allows you to show up as your best self in all areas of your life.

As we conclude this chapter on embracing abundance in every area of life, I invite you to reflect on the possibilities that lie before you. You have the power to create a life of abundance – one that goes beyond financial wealth and extends into every aspect of your being. Embrace gratitude, cultivate an abundance mindset, visualize your dreams, set clear goals, trust the process, seek supportive influences, and prioritize self-care. Remember, you deserve all the richness and abundance that life has to offer.

So, dear reader, as you continue your journey towards a wealthy mindset and the art of instantaneous gratitude, know that the path to abundance is always within your grasp. Embrace each day with open arms, choose abundance in every aspect of your life, and be ready to witness the miracles unfold. There is an abundant world waiting for you – are you ready to claim it?

Chapter 19: Leverage Your Mindset for Success

Success. It's a word that holds different meanings for different people. For some, success may mean climbing the corporate ladder and achieving financial prosperity. For others, it could be finding inner peace and fulfillment in their personal lives. Regardless of how you define success, one thing remains constant – your mindset plays a significant role in determining whether you achieve it or not.

In this chapter, we will explore the power of an abundant mindset and how it can be the foundation for achieving success in all areas of your life, from career to personal fulfillment. You see, scarcity and abundance are not merely concepts limited to material possessions; they are states of mind. When you shift from scarcity to abundance, you open up a world of opportunities and possibilities.

Let's delve deeper into the abundance mindset and its impact on your journey towards success. Imagine waking up every morning with a deep sense of gratitude for all the blessings in your life. Rather than focusing on what you lack, you appreciate what you already have. This attitude of gratitude creates a positive outlook that attracts more abundance into your life.

When you adopt an abundant mindset, you begin to see opportunities where others see obstacles. Instead of dwelling on limitations, you seek creative solutions and embrace a growth mindset. Challenges become stepping stones, failures turn into valuable lessons, and setbacks become fuel for progress.

One key aspect of an abundant mindset is the belief in your own worthiness and deservingness of success. You understand that success is not reserved for a select few, but rather, it is available to all who believe in themselves and are willing to put in the necessary work. This self-belief provides the confidence and motivation needed to pursue your goals relentlessly.

Furthermore, an abundant mindset allows you to embrace abundance in all its forms. It extends beyond material wealth and encompasses emotional, spiritual, and intellectual abundance. You value your relationships, prioritize self-care, and nurture your personal growth. By acknowledging the abundance present in your life already, you attract more abundance in all areas.

When you approach life with a mindset of abundance, you become a magnet for success. Opportunities seem to gravitate towards you, and you effortlessly attract the right people and resources to support your journey. Your positive energy and optimism become contagious, inspiring those around you and creating a ripple effect of abundance.

As you continue to cultivate your abundant mindset, you will notice a gradual transformation in your life. Your career may take unexpected turns that lead to greater fulfillment and prosperity. Your relationships will deepen and flourish, fueled by your ability to appreciate and celebrate the abundance within them. Your personal growth will soar as you embrace new challenges with unwavering faith in your abilities.

Remember, an abundant mindset is not something you achieve overnight. It requires consistent practice and conscious effort to rewire your thoughts and beliefs. Start by becoming aware of any scarcity-oriented patterns or negative self-talk that may be holding you back. Replace these limiting beliefs with affirmations of abundance and gratitude.

In the second half of this chapter, we will explore practical strategies to leverage your abundant mindset for success. We will dive into specific techniques that will empower you to attract abundance and manifest your goals. Get ready for a transformational journey that will unlock the doors to your limitless potential.

Stay tuned for the next part of this chapter, where we reveal the secrets to leveraging your abundant mindset for success. It's time to unleash the power within you and embrace a life of abundance and achievement. Get ready to take the next step on your journey towards true success.

Throughout the first half of this chapter, we have explored the power of an abundant mindset and its impact on achieving success in all areas of life. We have learned that abundance is not limited to material possessions, but rather a state of mind that opens up a world of opportunities and possibilities. By shifting our perspective from scarcity to abundance, we can attract more abundance into our lives.

Now, let's dive deeper into practical strategies to leverage your abundant mindset for success. These techniques will empower you to manifest your goals and unlock your limitless potential.

1. Practice Visualization:

Visualization is a powerful tool that allows you to create a clear mental image of your desired outcome. Take a few moments each day to visualize yourself achieving your goals and living a life of abundance. Picture the details, the emotions, and the impact it has on all aspects of your life. By consistently visualizing your success, you are programming your mind to attract and create the circumstances necessary to achieve it.

2. Gratitude Journaling:

Continuing the attitude of gratitude we discussed in the first half of this chapter, keeping a gratitude journal can be a transformative practice. Every day, write down at least three things you are grateful for. It could be a small accomplishment, a kind gesture from someone, or simply the beauty of nature around you. As you cultivate gratitude, you amplify the abundance already present in your life, attracting more blessings and opportunities.

3. Surround Yourself with Abundance:

Your environment significantly influences your mindset. Surround yourself with positive, like-minded individuals who support and inspire you. Seek out mentors or experts in your field who have achieved the level of success you aspire to. Their knowledge and encouragement will fuel your belief in your own abilities and inspire you to take bold steps towards your goals.

4. Set Realistic Goals:

While fostering an abundant mindset is essential for success, it's equally important to set realistic and achievable goals. Break down your larger, long-term goals into smaller, actionable steps. This way, you can celebrate milestones along the way, building momentum and motivation. Setting realistic goals allows you to track your progress and make adjustments as needed, ensuring steady progress towards the abundant life you envision.

5. Practice Self-Care:

Taking care of yourself is a vital aspect of an abundant mindset. Make self-care a priority by nourishing your mind, body, and soul. Engage in activities that bring you joy and help you relax. Prioritize activities that promote your mental and physical well-being, such as exercise, meditation, and hobbies. Remember, when you take care of yourself, you have more energy and clarity to pursue your goals and attract abundance into your life.

6. Embrace the Power of Affirmations:

Affirmations are positive statements that reinforce your belief in abundance and success. Create personalized affirmations that resonate with you and repeat them daily. Affirmations such as "I am worthy of all the abundance life has to offer" or "I attract opportunities that align with my vision" help reprogram your subconscious mind and build self-confidence. With consistent practice, positive affirmations become deeply ingrained in your mindset, empowering you to attract success and abundance effortlessly.

7. Take Inspired Action:

While maintaining an abundant mindset is crucial, it alone is not enough. You must also take inspired action towards your goals. Trust your intuition and listen to the inner nudges that guide you towards the right opportunities and actions. Push past your comfort zone, embrace challenges, and take calculated risks. Remember, abundance follows action, so seize every opportunity that aligns with your vision and keep moving forward.

As you integrate these practical strategies into your life, you will witness a transformation in your mindset and ultimately achieve success. Combine the power of visualization, gratitude journaling, surrounding yourself with abundance, setting realistic goals, practicing self-care, embracing affirmations, and taking inspired action. With each step, you will steadily unlock your true potential and create a life of abundance and achievement.

Remember, your abundant mindset is within your control. By consistently practicing these strategies, you will continue to expand your belief in possibilities, attract abundance, and achieve true success. Now, go forth and embrace the power of your abundant mindset. The world is waiting for you to shine your light and create a ripple effect of abundance in all areas of your life.

Chapter 20: Sharing Abundance: Paying It Forward

Imagine a world where acts of kindness and generosity abound, where everyone is connected through a common thread of gratitude and abundance. In this chapter, we delve deep into the concept of sharing abundance and explore the profound impact it can have on our lives and the world around us.

At the heart of sharing abundance lies the simple yet transformative act of giving back. When we have an abundance mindset, we realize that our wealth, whether it be financial or otherwise, is not meant to be hoarded but rather shared to create a positive ripple effect. It is about recognizing that by giving more, we receive more in return, not only in material terms but also in fulfillment, joy, and a profound sense of purpose.

One of the main reasons why sharing abundance is so important is because it helps break the cycle of scarcity that often plagues our lives. It is easy to get caught up in the mentality of always wanting more, constantly striving for the next big thing without ever feeling truly fulfilled. However, when we shift our focus from scarcity to abundance, we understand that true wealth lies not only in what we possess, but also in what we willingly give away.

When we share our abundance, whether it is our time, resources, or skills, we create a positive impact that extends far beyond ourselves. Consider the story of a successful entrepreneur who decides to invest in education programs for underprivileged children. By providing these children with opportunities they would not have otherwise had, she not only transforms their lives but also gives them the tools they need to create a brighter future for themselves and their communities. In doing so, she sets into motion a powerful ripple effect of positivity and change.

Sharing abundance also fosters a sense of interconnectedness and unity among individuals. When we realize that we are all part of a larger whole, we begin to understand that our actions, no matter how small, can make a significant difference. Whether it is volunteering at a local charity, donating to a worthy cause, or simply offering a helping hand to someone in need, each act of kindness has the potential to inspire others to do the same.

Moreover, sharing abundance allows us to tap into the power of gratitude. When we give selflessly, without expecting anything in return, we cultivate a deep sense of appreciation for what we have. This gratitude, in turn, opens the doors to even more abundance and blessings in our lives. As Melody Beattie once said, "Gratitude unlocks the fullness of life. It turns what we have into enough, and more. It turns denial into acceptance, chaos to order, confusion to clarity..."

So, if sharing abundance is so transformative and powerful, why is it often met with resistance? One reason is that many people operate from a scarcity mindset, fueled by fear and the belief in limited resources. In a world that is often driven by competition, it can be difficult to let go of the fear of not having enough. However, when we embrace the abundance mindset, we realize that there is more than enough to go around for everyone.

Another reason may be the misconception that one needs to have vast wealth or material possessions before they can start giving back. However, sharing abundance is not limited to financial resources alone. It can be as simple as offering a word of encouragement, sharing knowledge, or even lending a listening ear. Every act of kindness, no matter how small, has the power to create a ripple effect of positive change.

In the second half of this chapter, we will delve deeper into practical ways to share abundance and how it can enrich our lives. We will explore the different avenues through which we can contribute to positive change in both our immediate surroundings and on a larger scale. Get ready to embark on a journey of self-discovery and empowerment as we uncover the true impact of sharing abundance.

Let's pause here and reflect on the power of sharing abundance. The first half of this chapter has introduced us to the concept and its transformative potential. Now, let's dive into the practical ways in which we can start sharing abundance and creating a positive ripple effect in our world. Stay tuned for the second half of this chapter, where we will explore the actionable steps, we can take to make a difference. The journey towards a wealthy mindset built on instantaneous gratitude awaits us. In the second half of this chapter, we will explore practical ways to cultivate a mindset of sharing abundance and how it can enrich our lives and the lives of others. We will delve into the different avenues through which we can contribute to positive change in both our immediate surroundings and on a larger scale.

One powerful way to share abundance is through acts of kindness and generosity. These acts can range from simple gestures like offering a helping hand to a neighbor or colleague, to more significant contributions such as volunteering at a local charity or donating to a cause close to your heart. The key is to approach these acts with a genuine intention to make a positive impact, without expecting anything in return.

Consider the story of a woman named Emma who decided to make it a daily habit to perform random acts of kindness. She would start her day by leaving small notes of encouragement for her family members, colleagues, or even strangers she encountered throughout her day. This simple act of sharing abundance not only brightened the recipient's day but also brought immense joy and fulfillment to Emma herself. By consciously making the effort to spread kindness, she was able to create a ripple effect that touched the hearts of many.

Another avenue to share abundance is by sharing knowledge and skills. We all have unique talents and experiences that can be of benefit to others. Whether it's teaching a workshop, mentoring someone in your field, or simply taking the time to listen and give guidance, sharing your expertise can have a profound impact on someone's life. By empowering others with the tools and knowledge they need to thrive, you are contributing to a cycle of growth and abundance.

In addition to individual actions, collaborating with like-minded individuals or organizations can amplify the impact of sharing abundance. By joining forces, pooling resources, and working towards a common goal, we can create real change in our communities and beyond. This could involve participating in community projects, fundraising for a worthy cause, or even starting your own initiative to address a specific issue. The possibilities are endless when we come together with a shared vision and a commitment to making a difference.

Furthermore, embracing the concept of sharing abundance can extend beyond our immediate surroundings. It's important to recognize the interconnectedness of the world and to consider how our actions can benefit humanity as a whole. Supporting global initiatives, advocating for social justice, and promoting sustainability are all ways in which we can contribute to creating a more equitable and abundant world.

As we navigate the journey of sharing abundance, it's essential to remember that our actions may not always yield immediate results or visible changes. However, every act of kindness and generosity has the power to create a ripple effect. We may never fully grasp the extent to which our small actions can impact the lives of others and inspire them to pay it forward.

In conclusion, sharing abundance is a transformative practice that not only benefits others but also enriches our own lives. It breaks the cycle of scarcity, fosters unity, and taps into the power of gratitude. By embracing the abundance mindset and taking actionable steps to share our wealth, whether it be material, emotional, or intellectual, we can create a positive ripple effect that extends far beyond ourselves.

So, let's embark on this journey of self-discovery and empowerment as we uncover the true impact of sharing abundance. Together, let's create a world where acts of kindness and generosity abound, and where we all recognize the power, we have to make a difference. Get ready to experience the profound fulfillment that comes from living a life of abundant gratitude and sharing. The possibilities are limitless, and the world awaits the positive ripple effect we can create.

Disclaimer

The information provided in this book is for general informational and educational purposes only and is not intended as a substitute for professional advice, diagnosis, or treatment. The author and publisher have made every effort to ensure the accuracy and reliability of the information provided within these pages, but they make no guarantees, either express or implied, regarding the content's completeness, accuracy, or applicability.

Neither the author nor the publisher shall be held liable or responsible for any misunderstanding or misuse of the information contained in this book or for any loss, damage, or injury caused, or alleged to be caused, directly or indirectly by any treatment, action, or application of any advice discussed in this publication. The statements made within this book are not intended to diagnose, treat, cure, or prevent any disease. Readers should consult with a qualified healthcare provider for medical advice tailored to their personal circumstances.

The views and opinions expressed herein are those of the author alone and do not necessarily reflect the official policy or position of any agency or company. All content provided in this book is on an "as-is" basis and the author and publisher disclaim all responsibility for any errors or omissions.

Don't miss out!

Visit the website below and you can sign up to receive emails whenever Gonzalo Estrada publishes a new book. There's no charge and no obligation.

https://books2read.com/r/B-A-OZBBB-FBHZC

BOOKS 2 READ

Connecting independent readers to independent writers.

Also by Gonzalo Estrada

Self Healing
Visualiza tu Éxito
Cultivando Líderes
Afirmaciones y Empoderamiento
Semillas de Cambio
Cómo convertir TikTok en una máquina de hacer dinero
Cómo hacer dinero con Pinterest
Cómo hacer un ensayo
Cómo Pedir un Aumento de Sueldo
Currículo Poderoso
Entrenamiento sin Violencia
Entrevista Laboral
Gana Dinero con X (Twitter)
Ganar Masa Muscular
Volver a Empezar; el arte de reinventarse
Analiza Resuelve Ejecuta
Aromatherapy, The natural path to your pet´s well being
Holistic Feeding
The ABC of Educating Your Pet
The Art of Cosmic Connection
The Art of Feng Shui applied to your Pets
From Scarcity to Abundance
The English Bulldog in The Family
Therapeutic Massages for Pets